AN MBA'S GUIDE

to Self-Assessment
and Career Development

JAMES G. CLAWSON
*The Colgate Darden Graduate School
of Business Administration
University of Virginia*

DAVID D. WARD
General Mills, Inc.

AN MBA'S GUIDE

to Self-Assessment
and Career Development

Prentice-Hall, Englewood Cliffs, N.J. 07632

Library of Congress Cataloging-in-Publication Data

CLAWSON, JAMES G.
    An MBA's guide to self-assessment and career
development.

    1. Management—Vocational guidance. 2. Business—
Vocational guidance. 3. Master of business adminis-
tration degree. I. Ward, David (David D.) II. Title.
HD38.C53 1986   650'.023'73   85-12295
ISBN   0-13-566811-5

Editorial/production supervision
    and interior design: *Nancy G. Follender*
Cover design: *Ben Santora*
Manufacturing buyer: *Ed O'Dougherty*

Printed in the United States of America

10 9 8 7 6 5 4 3 2 1

ISBN 0-13-566811-5   01

Prentice-Hall International (UK) Limited, *London*
Prentice-Hall of Australia Pty. Limited, *Sydney*
Prentice-Hall Canada Inc., *Toronto*
Prentice-Hall Hispanoamericana, S.A., *Mexico*
Prentice-Hall of India Private Limited, *New Delhi*
Prentice-Hall of Japan, Inc., *Tokyo*
Prentice-Hall of Southeast Asia Pte. Ltd., *Singapore*
Editora Prentice-Hall do Brasil, Ltda., *Rio de Janeiro*
Whitehall Books Limited, *Wellington, New Zealand*

We dedicate this book to our wives,
Susan Clawson and Sharon Ward,
for their support and encouragement
during its creation.

CONTENTS

FOREWORD

Jim Clawson and Dave Ward have done what many academicians in the fields of career development and self-assessment hope someday to do. They have written a truly useful book which can assist MBA students and others to pull together in a very short time some valuable information about themselves as prospective professionals in selected functional areas.

Clawson and Ward's book is valuable because it responds to a need, a need by MBAs to know how to decide on an entry-level position, and that need is strong. Recent demographic, social, and economic forces have created a national work force of people who have greater needs for self-fulfillment in their work. They are striving to win one of the fewer high-paying/high-status management positions available in today's market. Because of demand of these jobs, the desire of entering workers to make the right career fit has intensified. Today's young people want to broaden their career planning. They are intent on having their careers express their individual talents, values, and interests.

Those of us who study careers applaud this expanding interest in career planning on the part of students and would encourage them to spend the time to find their career fit, instead of allowing their careers to be determined by external opinions and pressures. For example, society in general leads them to believe they will be happy in a career if they work for the "right" organization, if they make a lot of money, or if they rise to the top very rapidly. Unfortunately these routes do not necessarily guarantee happiness. I have interviewed hundreds of people who achieved the above results and yet were very frustrated in their careers. The question then arises—what do they do to avoid being trapped in jobs that do not help them achieve their own objectives?

An MBA's Weekend Guide to Self-Assessment and Career Development provides an exciting answer. Clawson and Ward's techniques of self-evaluation will help many MBA's to avoid the negative consequences of uninformed entry-level choices. They will help them to avoid the tendency to move from one organization to another in an effort to find that illusive "career fit," thereby avoiding an undesirable reputation of being indecisive. Also, they will avoid the trap of feeling that things will get better after the first few years if they will just hang on and make it through the first bad time. The book also provides step-by-step procedures that will save the reader many hours of frustration later when a career sours or the recognition of a mistake in choice becomes apparent.

The second invaluable time-saver in the *MBA's Guide* is the "Job Research Reports," in which the authors have has collected 64 reports which contain fourteen functional job descriptions and fifty industry descriptions. The standardized format allows quick comparison between fields, and the depth of research, provided by student groups, represents more time than any one graduating MBA could spend.

This book, has greatly reduced the amount of time necessary for an MBA to do a quick match of his or her talents and interests with entry-level positions. The book will, in sum, make it possible for many MBAs to take a hard, focused look at data about themselves and about entry-level positions in order to follow a more intelligently-planned career path. I recommend it to anyone who is serious about a career.

Dr. Paul H. Thompson
Dean, School of Management
Brigham Young University

PREFACE

Many scholars and managers have focused their attention in the last ten years on the organizational career development process. Most of them seem to agree that the notion of FIT between an individual's characteristics and the characteristics of the job are central to success, for both the individual and the corporation. But the *fit* model has some difficulties. First, it demands an ability to describe the relevant parts (individuals, jobs, and organizations) along dimensions that relate to subsequent success. It is not clear to me that we have been able to identify what those dimensions are. Studies of managerial behavior vary widely in the *key* characteristics they highlight, and all of the internal studies that I have seen yield widely varying, very complex lists of essential dimensions. Furthermore, these dimensions must be consistent across the relevant parts. It makes little sense, in the fit model, to assess interpersonal style in an individual if one has no data on the interpersonal requirements of the job or on the interpersonal rules of the organization.

Second, the fit model assumes an ability to assess those dimensions in all of the relevant parts. Psychological testing, "systematic" job descriptions, and organizational diagnosis techniques have left us with a very imprecise body of skills for making these assessments. We have done better with individual assessment, but many of the techniques are time-consuming, subject to inaccuracies, and costly. We need more accurate, easily used, and inexpensive means of making these assessments.

Third, the fit model as it is usually characterized is a static model that assumes little or no change in the relevant parts. People, jobs, and organizations all change over time, so that even if we did know what dimensions to look at and had a means of assessing them, our assessments would grow all-too-quickly obsolete unless we updated them regularly. This is another reason we need relatively quick, efficient, and inexpensive tools for career development that can be used regularly.

The fit model, with all of its problems, is widely accepted. The innovative, award-winning course entitled "Self-Assessment and Career Development" developed by Tony Athos, Rod Hodgins, John Kotter, Victor Faux, and Charles MacArthur introduced at the Harvard Business School in the early 1970s was based on it; since then many schools have begun offering similar courses. The fit model works, helps people gain skill and confidence in career development, and provides a framework for attacking career development problems.

The need to describe both individuals and jobs that the model creates presents a practical problem, however. While teaching the Self-Assessment and Career Development course, I felt increasing pressure to provide information on the available job opportunities that was as sophisticated and detailed as the information students had generated in the course on themselves. I had nothing to offer. There were a number of haphazard attempts to summarize some characteristics of various career paths, but nothing satisfied the students. They were well-armed with personal information, but were constrained from using it as effectively as they wanted because they didn't have enough information on jobs to sift through.

So I asked them to do JOB RESEARCH REPORTS on jobs of their choosing. I collected these for four years and with David Ward and Margie Jernigan standardized them into the reports contained here. The reports reflect the jobs and the things about those jobs that MBA students wanted to know. And since they researched jobs that interested them, the reports were more than academic exercises for them. We used photocopies of these reports for several years as reference works on reserve in the library. Other students heard about them and began using them more and more.

Then these students realized that they didn't have the personal information they needed to assess fit with jobs, so they began coming to my office saying that they couldn't take the course, and they needed a shorter, similar self-assessment experience that could guide them in their job search. The second edition of *Self-Assessment and Career Development* was intended to be a full-blown version of the course that could be used off-the-shelf by individuals who had the determination to follow-through on the arduous experience the course provides. These students, however, didn't want a three-month answer; they and their friends wanted a three-day-or-less answer.

The repeatedly expressed need to have a shorter self-assessment exercise pushed us to include a brief section on self-assessment at the beginning of the book. The process outlined in Chapter 2 is much less rigorous than the full-blown process presented in the second edition of *Self-Assessment and Career Development*, but it will produce a very usable self-assessment. Given the number of student inquiries about writing cover letters and resumes, we have also included a chapter each on them.

This book was intended primarily to provide the kind of job/occupational information that students needed to match up with their self-assessment information—and to do that on dimensions that corresponded with the dimensions used in the course: cognitive style, interpersonal style, lifestyle, and orientation. The second edition of *Self-Assessment and Career Development* and this book are really companion volumes in that the former focuses on the self-assessment process and the latter focuses on the job assessment process, both essential elements of the fit model.

The volume of job opportunities suggested that once both individual and job had been described in related terms, the seemingly simple screening process of comparing a self-assessment with job characteristics to find those that promised a high level of fit would, alone, be a tremendous task. So we developed the simple grid that appears at the beginning of each job report as a means of facilitating that effort. These grids are intended as preliminary screens only and are not designed to reveal the goodness of fit in a comprehensive fashion. They are useful for screening job opportunities to find those that might be worthy of more detailed investigation.

The result is, we believe, a book that anyone seeking a job in the business world can use, first in a weekend to develop a relatively systematic self-assessment and second to develop a focus, based on that self-assessment, of job/career areas to pursue in their job search. We recognize the dynamic nature of individuals and of jobs—and encourage readers to advise us of changes in the information contained in the reports for future editions. Above all, our hope is that the book will be useful for many people seeking to understand themselves, their jobs, and the relationship between them better.

James G. Clawson
Charlottesville, Virginia

ACKNOWLEDGMENTS

We acknowledge on the following pages the students of the Harvard Business School and the Darden Graduate School of Business (UVA) classes whose reports contributed to this book. We also wish to note the efforts of Donna Sager, Nina Hutchinson, Kathleen Collier, and Judy Childress whose typing and reviewing of the manuscript were of great benefit. Marjorie Jernigan, Bill Van Doren, Gail Brown, and Bette Collins, also, were of great assistance in the final editing.

We also thank the Research Committee and the Sponsors of the Darden School for their support in this project.

A great many people have helped us prepare this book. Most of the information on specific job functions and industries was gathered by MBA students from the Harvard Business School and the Darden School at the University of Virginia. We would like to thank the following for their assistance:

Harvard Class of 1980:

Robert Agresta, Gerardo Angulo, Joan Aronson, Stephen Bailey, Jean Barron, Ivy Barton, Howard Baskin, George Beitzel, Robert Belden, Sheryle Bolton, Lester Bradshaw, Leonard Brandt, Carleton Bryant III, Tim Butler, Christopher Butler, Daniel Chasins, F. J. Chu, Raul Companioni, Paul Connolly, Eliav Dahan, Dwight Davidson, Rick Davis, Daniel Dickson, W. Dirlam, Thomas Downey, James Ducker, Tom Fischgrund, Richard Flaye, William Folger, Linda Frackman, Dwight Gertz, Robert Goehrke, Rachid Ghozali, John Goldman, Michael Goldman, Alisa Gravitz, Paul Gudonis, John Halenda, John Harbison, Frances Harris, Craig Harrison, Albert Holman III, Kristine Holland, Howard Hoople, Doranne Hudson, Elaine Ide, Karen Jacobson, Brian James, James Janke, Margaret Johns, Dara Jwaideh, Neil Jones, John Keenan, Michael Klaus, Laurence E. Landrigan, Catherine LeBlanc, Diedre Leopold, Donald Leopold, William Luden, Nancy Lukitsh, Robert Lusardi, Leigh Marriner, Allen Martin, Bonnie McFarland, Paige Meili, Cornelia Mitchell, Win Miller, Ellen Moran, Hope Neiman, Daniel O'Brien, Patricia O'Connell, Gary Phillips, Gary Polodna, Thomas Pyle, Mark Rahmel, W. Mason Rees, Lee Rimsky, John Risko, Michael Robbins, A. J. Robinson, Peter Russo, Joan Sapir, Jane S. Sacasa, Guy Schwartz, Mark Schwartz, Allen Shifflet, Thomas Sinkovic, Kenneth Snyder, John Stacey, Steven Steinhilber, William Stevens, Paul Theil, Faye Tiano, David Tolmie, Susan Thomas, Raymond Thompson, John Vogel, Hsueh-wei Wang, James Warner, Ronald Waugh, C. Martin Webber, Craig Whitehouse, and Russell Whittenburg.

Harvard Class of 1981:

Anthony Alaimo, Joseph Adams, Andrew Alisberg, Mark Antle, Barbara Apple, Roger Bell, Gary Bengier, Lincoln Berkely, Daniele Bevilacqua, Jeffrey

Bodenstab, Mary Bosco, Margaret Brady, Luise Bruan, Joel Bresler, Alice Brown, Judson Byrn, Rory Cowan, Damianos Damianos, Michael Delfiner, Barbara Deck, Carol DeVoort, Paul Donaher, James Dowling, John Edelmann, William Feltus, Michael Fitzgerald, David Fisher, Richard Flaye, Sally Foster, William Fowler III, Robyn Frey, G. Van Geyn, Robin Glantz, Carrie Gonzales-Rivas, Peter Gooneus, Timothy Grogan, Antonio Guijarro, Ben-Zion Guz, Herbert Hogue, Charles Honnet, Alice Howard, Bernard James, William Jefferis, Kimberly Jimenez, Susan Karash, Lisa Katzenstein, Sandra Keys, Kimberly Kispert, Kevin Kilgammon, Robin Krasny, John Krasznekewicz, John Lacey, Jeanne Liedtka, Robert Loomis, Stanton Marcus, Peter Mindnich, Kevin McCall, Mary McClure, James McGrath, Robert McKeeman, Bruce McNair, Paul Messinger, Michael Meyer, Rawle Michelson, David Millison, Peter Mills, Steven Mintz, Robert Montgomery, Alice Mozely, Alexander Nedzel, John Nielson, Michael Nightingale, Rita Ormasa, Luis Orozco, Richard Palmer, Beverly Patton, Nolan Perreira, Hollis Polk, D.L. Presser, Bruce Quackenbush, Jonathan Rolnick, Michael Rose, Peter Rule, Katherine Russell, Jane Sacasa, Susan Santon, Rin Sasaki, Jewel Savadelis, Liliana Scagliotti, Randy Schafer, Philippe Ullens de Schooten, Paul Schnoebelen, Ronald Serrano, William Sewell, Eileen Shapiro, Peter Martins da Silva, Thomas Shull, Nancy Smith, Karen Stephens, Sarah Stevens, Christopher Stix, Patrick Sullivan, Carmen Suro-Bredie, Christoph Tiefenbacher, Jean Tison, Mary Toman, Craig Triplett, Ronald Waugh, Theodore Wieber, Dorothy Wilmot, Lauren Wright, Margaret Young, Margaret Yates, Paul Zilk, and Vicki Zimet.

Harvard Class of 1982:

Marjorie Aldrich, Jerry Anping, Barrie Atkin, Howard Bartlett, Courtney Ann Behm, Mark Belinsky, Stephen Boucher, David Breecker, Charles Callan, Greg Costley, Nicholas Craw, David Crane, Richard Darer, James Dowd, Linda Dunn, Allison Elwers, Jane Ferguson, Philip Gianos, Linda Greene, Fredric Gross, Robert Halperin, Lorraine Hariton, William Harrison, Ralph James, Yousef Javadi, James Johnson, Julie Johnson, Keith Karnofsky, Elizabeth Kennedy, Carie Kennedy, Shafiq Kahn, Kathryn Knauss, Marie Konstance, Steven Kolodin, Dorothy Krauklis, Peter Maglothlin, Ina Mandel, Robert McKown, Dermot McMeekin, Jules McNeff, Jay Misra, Sandy Mobley, Stephen Necessary, Glenn Noveen, Bill Novak, Janet Ozarchuk, Sally Parnell, Smita Patel, Dyan Porter, Dan Richards, Fern Segerlind, Bill Sharman, Joan Straub, Janet Strauss, Morris Stockburger, Morely Thompson, Elsa Vidal, James Whelan, Betsey Whitbeck, Ennis Whitehead, Elizabeth Wilson, Philip Wong, and Lex Zaharoff.

Darden Class of 1982:

Glenn Camp, Deborah Carter, Soo Bong Choi, R. S. Creighton, Marion Dines, Dreika Degraff, Steven Durham, David Kelso, Missy Kilroy, Michael Kines, Sally Loving, Ruth Miller, Ross Mulford, Ben Parks, E. Clorissa Phillips,

E.J. Pipkin, John Reilly, Kevin Sachs, Robert Shumacher, Earl Seekins, Martin Sherrod, David Tew, Brigid Thompson, and Holly Whitin.

We would also like to thank Mark Pacala for his comments on the Consulting industry, Dan J. Person and Jeff Diamond of the Prudential Insurance Company of America for their comments on HMOs and the Insurance industry, Benjamin K.B. Young for his assistance on International Banking, George Duke (Darden '83) for his assistance on Accounting, Kevin Ingely (Darden '83) for his help on the Hotel Industry, Chip Lilley (Darden '83) for his contribution to Real Estate, C. Madison Reilly for his help on Retailing, and Charles Ward for his contribution to Sales. Thanks, too, to Jeff Sonnenfeld (HBS) for his help in collecting the data from the HBS class of '82. Finally, Joseph Collins Smith II, Ed Hawfield, and Ned Case helped with aspects of the final draft.

Part 1

INTRODUCTION

A variety of universities have, in recent years, begun offering courses on career management, some of which are modeled after the Self-Assessment and Career Development (SACD) course taught at the Harvard Business School between 1978 and 1981 and most recently the career management courses taught at the Colgate Darden Graduate School of Business Administration at the University of Virginia. The SACD course was a demanding but popular one that required students to generate, analyze, and act upon over a hundred pages of personal data. After three months of work, SACD students emerged with a detailed personal profile, a list of the implications of that profile for the kind of work they should be seeking, and a specific plan to guide them during their job search. SACD students said that they were much better prepared than they otherwise would have been to manage their own careers and the careers of others, and to apply the essential managerial skills of inductive logic, planning, and adaptation.

Every year, other people, hearing about the course and the testimonials of those who had taken it, would come to the faculty and say something like

> I'm very interested in your careers course, but I couldn't find room in my schedule to do such an extensive project. I now find that I'm faced with a lot of uncertainty about myself and the kind of work I should be seeking. Can you give me some guidance? I am willing to spend a weekend or maybe four or five days working on this, and then I need to be making some strategic decisions about what I'm going to do.

The cynical response to these inquiries would be that people should not really try to make such important decisions in such a limited time, but that would not change the realities. People do find themselves faced with major decisions and insufficient data and not much time. So we compressed the semester-long process outlined in *Self-Assessment and Career Development* (also published by Prentice-Hall, second edition, 1985) in the first part of this book in an attempt to answer those requests. This book first sets out a program that will develop useful information about yourself in one or two weekends of devoted effort. The program does not guarantee that you will find answers to all questions about yourself or that you will find your perfect job or that you will make the right decisions. It will, however, provide a systematic approach for you to obtain information on a variety of personal dimensions, which you can then use to screen and to decide upon various career- and job-related opportunities that come to you or that you develop.

Job Research Reports

There is and has been a need for something more than the self-assessment guide, however. We have found that students typically felt comfortable and confident about their self-assessment exercises and conclusions, but then needed comparable information about organizations and entry-level MBA job positions that matched the sophistication and detail of their personal data. Students were unable to find in any one source a relevant and comprehensive profile of the various kinds of job positions that greeted MBA graduates.

The second part of the book, therefore, is intended to provide a quick reference guide to a variety of MBA entry-level job positions. This will help job hunters to match their personal profiles quickly with the profiles of various entry-level positions.

These job profiles were developed over the course of four years by students at the Harvard Business School and at the Darden Business School in an exercise called *Job Research Reports.* In these assignments, students were asked to identify a particular job that was of interest to them and to gather information about it. We have standardized those reports from the last three years and include them here.

The data contained in these reports are primarily the work of students enrolled in these career management courses. We have recognized their efforts earlier in the Acknowledgments. For the most part, we have let the data stand without more than format modifications. We fully expect that some pieces of information will be incomplete, possibly inconsistent with the rest of the reports in the book, or perhaps growing obsolete. Consequently, we expect the book to be an ongoing reference work that will be continually updated in the future. To those of you who are working in—or who have had experience recruiting in—particular areas outlined in the book and who find inconsistencies or inaccuracies, we encourage you to tear out one of the forms at the end of the book and send it to us for inclusion in the next edition. Feel free, too, if you like, to telephone (804-924-7486) to pass on information more quickly.

Actively managing your career is not easy. Even the brief and rough approximation of the Self-Assessment and Career Development course given here will require a good deal of work and introspection, but the confidence and purposefulness you can gain from a careful self-assessment will be worth much more than the effort. The ability subsequently to check your findings against job profiles will make your own profile a powerful instrument of career development.

1 AN MBA'S WEEKEND GUIDE TO SELF-ASSESSMENT

We encourage you to prepare to work through this self-assessment process by eliminating the possibilities of distraction. One way to do this is to go away from your usual surroundings. Rent a hotel or resort room out of town for the weekend; do not take phone calls or worry about things like mowing the grass or doing homework. Concentrating your efforts and removing the routine clutter from your life will clear your thoughts and feelings and will improve your data.

You will need some writing equipment and a good supply of paper. Purchase some 8½'' × 11'' lined, punched paper and a three-ring binder in which you can keep your self-assessment and career development materials, notes, and ideas—not only for now, but also for the future. It is difficult to learn *from* yourself *about* yourself over time if your notes are disorganized. You will need ten or more index tabs to organize your material. Also, bring your daily appointment book, if you keep one regularly, and, if you have a resume, bring it along, too.

Once you have selected a two-day period and have readied yourself (don't forget a good night's sleep), work slowly through the steps that follow.

Step 1: Previous Jobs

Take a sheet of paper and write the name of the last job that you held at the top of both the front and back of the sheet of paper. Working backward in time, make a separate sheet of paper for each and every job you have held. Include part-time or summer work. Once you have completed titling on both sides, stack the pages in chronological order with the last job on top. Then go through the stack one at a time, writing on the *front* of the page one-line descriptions of the things you *liked* about each job.

Feel free to repeat yourself. In other words, if you liked the freedom or autonomy that you had in several jobs, write that down on each page where it applies. Just because you have written a characteristic once, do not skip writing it on other pages if those jobs also had that attractive feature.

Press yourself to think of all the things you liked about each job. Be thorough and try not to take anything for granted. Think about the rewards— monetary and nonmonetary—the people you worked with, the flexibility or control over your time, the activities that were involved with that job, the people you met pursuing that job, its proximity to your home, and so on.

Once you have listed all the things you liked about each job, turn the stack over and begin writing the things that you disliked about each job. Again, be as specific as you can. Feel free to name names and to note specific incidents that you did not like. Again, repeat yourself when it is appropriate; if the same thing irritated you about three different jobs, write it down on those three different pieces of paper. When you have listed the things that you did not like about each job, put this set of papers in your binder under an index entitled "Previous Jobs."

Step 2: People

Take a sheet of paper and at the top of the page write "People." On the front of the page, write the things that you like about other people. Think of all the characteristics of your friends, your associates, and the people you have met who impress you or appeal to you. One way to do this is to write down a person's name, think about that person, and note all of his or her characteristics that you like. When you have completed noting the things that you like about people (did it take more than one page?), turn the pages over and do the same for the things that you do *not* like about people. Put these pages in your notebook under a tab marked "People."

Step 3: Time

Your objective in this step is to create a time allocation chart, a record of the way you spent your time during the last ten days. If you keep an appointment book, consult it for this step. Title a sheet of paper "Time Analysis." On the left-hand side, write all the different things you did during the last ten days—for instance, sleeping, eating, personal hygiene (showering, combing your hair, dressing), traveling and commuting, work activities, recreational activities, talking to other people, attending sports events, and so on.

If you write "work" or "school" or any other general activity, break it down into more detailed components. Under "work," for instance, you might write "working alone at a desk," "working on the telephone with other people," "working in meetings," and so forth. Under "school" you might write down "in class," (noting what the classes were), "studying," or "snoozing." Make this list of activities as detailed and as specific as you can. Try to look at 15-minute intervals in order to press yourself into careful descriptions of what you did. This exercise will take some time, so relax, reflect, and do not hurry through it. If you feel that the last ten days were not typical of the way you spend your time, make a time log for the previous ten days or the ten days before that. Choose any ten days you like and do the exercise to find out how you spend your time.

On the right-hand side of the page count up all the hours you spent in each activity. The total at the bottom of the page must equal 240 hours, or 24 hours times 10 days. At this point, you will have a list of activities on the left-hand side of the page and, on the right-hand side, a list of hours spent on each activity summed to 240 at the bottom.

Now calculate the percentage of your time spent in each activity. Write these percentages next to the hour figure for each activity. Finally, put these data in your notebook under "Time."

This exercise gives you an idea of how you actually spend your time. Given that we all have the same resources (240 hours of time and the freedom to choose what to do with it), this tabulation gives you a behavioral perspective on your values. Frequently we lose track of what we do and wonder where the time went, especially since we have so many things to do. A "time-spent" inventory like this will help you to see more clearly the relationship between your values, goals, and desires and what you actually do. In the final analysis, what we *do* is what we *are*.

You may not feel you had any control over your activities during the ten-day period. Not true. At some point, you *chose* to be every place you were, and those choices reflect a great deal about your values and goals.

Step 4: Coursework

On the front of a sheet of paper entitled "Classes," list the classes in school that you enjoyed most. Then note the reasons why you enjoyed them. On the back of the paper, list the classes that you enjoyed the least and reasons why. Was it the school, the text, the subject matter, the teacher—and if so, what about him or her?—and so on. This page goes under the tab "Coursework."

Step 5: Skills

On another sheet of paper list the things that you believe you can do well—that is, your "Skills." What are the mental, physical, emotional, and interpersonal activities in which you feel well qualified and capable? Force yourself to write down *every-thing* that you can think of. Sometimes people have a difficult time identifying their own good points. To help do this step, ask yourself what others compliment you on. They may say that you are good with people, have an outgoing personality, are good at typing or at analyzing financial figures; whatever they may be, write down your list of skills on the front of the page. (Later, you will be asking people who know you to add to the list.)

Then, on the back of the page, list the things that you are not very good at. Note the big mistakes you have made and why. Include any fears you may have that affect your behavior. One woman, for instance, was afraid of flying in airplanes and realized that this fear would rule out her taking a job in management consulting.

By now it is probably time to take a break. Stop for a while and take a walk or go for a workout and then eat lunch. When you return, reread the work you have done so far and make additions: Fill in the gaps, refine descriptions, write in the things you just remembered while you were out. Be as complete as you can.

Step 6: Life Themes

By this time you have compiled a fairly multidimensional look at some of your major characteristics. Your task now is to use those five sets of data to generate a list of related personal characteristics or "Life Themes."

A Life Theme is a simple, concise description of an aspect of who you are. One way to think about writing these themes is to complete the sentence, "I am a person who _____." You might say for instance, "I am a person who feels un-comfortable meeting new people in new situations." Or "I am a person who is un-comfortable meeting people in new situations at the start, but who makes friends later."

Where do these Life Themes come from? From the data you have been generating all day. To compose your Life Themes, flip through the sheets you have written and try to identify the patterns that run through several of them. Let the data speak. Try not to impose your preconceived conclusions about yourself, even though they may be accurate; rather, pull together connected pieces of evidence that have a common thread. As you think about and look back over the things you have written—look for the patterns that describe who you *are*—not who you want to be, or who you once were, but who you are *now*.

In some cases you may notice trends that indicate you are enjoying or liking certain things more and more and perhaps liking other things less and less. Note these trends as well as the patterns of what you are.

Figure 1-1 outlines a number of areas to consider as you develop your list of Life Themes. See if your data reveal any themes in each of the areas outlined in Figure 1-1.

Number each theme you develop and insert it under "Life Themes" in your notebook. Collecting these themes may take the rest of the day; do not try to rush the process.

Life Theme labels that will be of use to you have several common characteristics. First, each one reflects a volume of data. If you have developed Life Themes from only one or two bits of data, you are probably trying to impose an interpretation on them that is not supported.

Second, good labels are simple. Lengthy labels are more confusing than helpful. However, single-word labels are generally too broad to be useful.

Effective labels will also be specific and varied. General labels that say the same thing in different words will constrain your ability to review a variety of job opportunities.

Use the foregoing criteria to judge the quality of your labels and refine them as

Figure   1-1

PERSONAL DIMENSIONS TO CONSIDER IN WRITING LIFE THEMES

Physical	Professional
Intellectual	Educational
Emotional	Financial
Spiritual/philosophical	Material
Social	Recreational
Marital	Societal
Familial	Ecclesiastical

Note: Feel free to include other areas or aspects of your life as you write your list of personal characteristics. You may feel that other categories (such as "aesthetic") should be included for your survey of personal characteristics to be comprehensive.

you work through them repeatedly. Figures 1-2 and 1-3 show some well-written and useful Life Themes. Note how they relate to the several areas listed in Figure 1-1. Note, too, how they are concise and specific.

When you have developed a list that seems comprehensive to you, go through it again and assign priorities to your themes. Write an "A" by those themes that are most important. Then write a "C" by those themes that are least important or do not cause you to feel strongly, namely, those themes upon which you could compromise. Finally, write a "B" beside the rest of your themes. Now rewrite your themes listing them in order of priority, grouping the "A' s," "B's," and "C's" together (see Figure 1-3).

Once you have identified and listed your Life Themes, call it a day. Get some rest. There is more to do tomorrow.

Figure   1-2

ALEXANDER HATHAWAY'S LIFE THEMES

I am a person who . . .

1.   Is strongly influenced by my father.
2.   Has a high need for prestige and recognition.
3.   Loves people socially, not benevolently.
4.   Prefers an easygoing environment.
5.   Prefers an organized, stable environment.
6.   Dislikes academics.
7.   Is very goal oriented—shoots for the top.
8.   Loves to entertain—has a strong sense of humor.
9.   Is concerned about how others view me.
10.   Enjoys reading about and watching sports.
11.   Is future oriented—likes to think about what is coming.
12.   Needs to feel responsible for work.
13.   Feels that family is important—needs to see them often.
14.   Enjoys traveling.
15.   Likes to make overall pictures from smaller details.
16.   Needs positive feedback and support regularly.
17.   Takes the easy way out if there is high chance of failure.
18.   Enjoys dealing with superiors or elders.
19.   Has confidence in my personality.
20.   Takes a realistic approach to problems.

Figure   1-3

JEWEL SAVADELIS'S LIFE THEMES

I am a person who . . .

Dominant Themes

1. Likes to be in control.
2. Has self-confidence.
3. Likes dealing with people.
4. Needs husband's support.

Major Themes

5. Deals well with people.
6. Wants to achieve significant ends and to improve self.
7. Is creative and appreciates aesthetics.
8. Is risk loving.
9. Needs praise and recognition.
10. Can get things accomplished.
11. Needs self-respect.
12. Likes variety.
13. Is emotional.

Intermediate Themes

14. Is flexible.
15. Has high material needs.
16. Needs support of friends and family.
17. Lacks stamina.
18. Is self-reliant.
19. Is concerned about the position of women in life.
20. Is organized.
21. Is intuitive.

Subordinate Themes

22. Is conventional.
23. Is impatient.
24. Is practical.

Copyright © 1980 by the Cologate Darden Graduate Business School Sponsors, Charlottesville, VA. From the case "Jewel Savadelis (A)," UVA-OB-190, by James G. Clawson. Reprinted by permission.

Step 7: Goals

In the morning, take four pieces of paper and, at the top of one page, write "One-Year Goals"; at the top of the next page write "Three-Year Goals"; at the top of the third page, write "Ten-Year Goals"; and at the top of the last page, "Thirty-Year

Goals." These pages are to contain descriptions of what you would like to have or do or *be* 1,3,10, and 30 years in the future.

In the left-hand margin of each of these pages, write the words that are on the list in Figure 1-1. You may not have a lot of certainty or clarity about what you want to do, have, or be in 10 or 30 years, but try to think about the future in a systematic way. Across the top of each page, write "Have," "Have Done," and "Be." The pages will now look like the one in Figure 1-4.

Write down the things you would like to have (own), have done, or be in each of those areas in 1,3,10, and 30 years. Be as specific as you can. Do not worry that these goals may change, as they certainly will. You are only trying to establish a tentative, forward-looking plan for guiding your activities. When you are done, put these papers in your notebook under "Goals."

Step 8: Implications

You have a rank-ordered list of personal characteristics (Life Themes) and a list of goals at various points in the future. Your job now is to develop from these two lists a set of "Implications" for the kind of work you should be seeking. This list must be directly and closely tied to your list of personal themes and personal goals.

As you list the Implications, include reference to particular themes or bits of data from the earlier data-generating exercises. This practice will force you to make sure that your Implications are closely tied to data or themes that you have written

Figure   1-4

Goals for _____ Years from Now (19_____)			
I want to			
Dimensions	Have	Have Done	Be
Physical			
Intellectual			
Spiritual/philosophical			
Emotional			
Marital			
Familial			
Social			
Societal			
Recreational			
Professional			
Financial			
Material			
Educational			
Ecclesiastical			

before. If you cannot identify a specific theme or a goal that relates directly to the Implication that you are writing, leave it out. An unrelated Implication is an illogical jump and means that you are responding to the expectations of other people, or of society, or of your own ideal view of "success" rather than to your own current characteristics and goals. Figure 1-5 outlines some areas that may stimulate your thinking.

Implications can be worded most productively if you write them so that they will complete the sentence, "I should be seeking work that _____." For example, if you had a theme—and it was, say, Number 7 in your Life Theme list—that reads, "I like to work alone," one implication of that theme would be, "I should be seeking work that will not require that I work constantly with a lot of other peo-

Figure   1-5

DIMENSIONS OF IMPLICATIONS FOR WORK

Daily Tasks

What kinds of things do you like to do each day? How much variety do you need in each day's activities? How much physical action do you need in each day's activities? What kind of mental problems would you like to be solving?

Dealing with Fellow Employees

How much autonomy do you need? How many people would you like to work with? Are you able to rely on other people to give you the information or work that you need in order to complete your own work? How friendly are you with people on the job? What kinds of people would you like to work with? What kinds of people would you not like to work with?

Dealing with Other People

How much contact would you like with the public? In what kind of arrangement? Would you like to be selling? Would you like to be responding to their requests?

Time Management

How much control do you want over your use of time? How fast do you work? How do you respond to time pressure? Deadlines? How many hours a week do you want to work? How willing are you to adapt your schedule to variations in work time? What about overtime on evenings and weekends?

Cognitive Style

How do you think? Do you take a sequential approach to solving problems or do you prefer to look at all of the data at once? Do you prefer to look at the big picture or are you more interested in working with the details? Do you spend large amounts of time on a problem or do you prefer to have several things going at once and to "check in" with each problem intermittently?

ple." After writing that Implication, you could write (T7) to remind you of its connection to your themes. There may be other themes that would give the same indication, and you could include them in your reference as well. This referencing, again, is important because it presses you to connect your Implications to your data. Figure 1-6 presents some well-written Implications.

You are probably a little drained from all of this reflection and writing. If you

Figure 1-6

JEWEL SAVADELIS'S IMPLICATIONS

Company Style

1. Company should be renegade in its thinking. (T8, T21, T14, T7, T11, T22)
2. Company should permit employees time to devote to outside activities and not be workaholic. (T4, T16, T1, T17)
3. Company should encourage personal growth and advancement. (T13, T12, T6, T9)
4. Company should provide open access to all levels of executives. (T13, T12, T6, T5)
5. Corporate executives should be fair and ethical leaders. (T11, T19)
6. Company should value its employees. (T15, T1, T18)
7. Company should provide pleasant physical surroundings. (T15, T1, T6, T8)
8. Company should operate for profit and manufacture a tangible product or service. (T24)

Life-style

9. Life-style should permit time for self: for philosophizing, for intellectual growth, for professional growth, and for physical maintenance. (T11, T2, T6, T3, T12)
10. Life-style should include time for spouse and family. (T4, T16)
11. Life-style should include time for social and recreational activities. (T7, T16, T8, T20)
12. Life-style should include time for societal needs. (T19)
13. Life should take place in an attractive location. (T12, T14, T7, T19, T8, T4)

Relationships with People at Work

14. People with whom I work should be diverse with at least a few sharing my values and traits. (T12, T5)
15. My boss should be nonauthoritarian. (T1, T6, T11, T9)
16. Although I am able to deal with many diverse people (T5, T12), I may be lonely without a few peers with whom I can share experiences. They should be nonrigid (T14), bright (T13), and unconventional (T12, T22) and have integrity (T11)
17. People with whom I work should create an open, informal atmosphere with easygoing relationships. (T2, T5, T12)
18. I expect to be treated with respect, honesty, and encouragement. (T2, T5, T11)
19. I prefer to organize and lead groups in which authority is ambiguous. (T5, T20, T9)

20. I prefer to motivate people by challenging them and dealing with them fairly. (T6, T5, T14)
21. I demand that each team member pull his or her share. (T18, T23)
22. I will work to achieve organizational goals. (T20, T24, T8, T22)

Job Characteristics

23. Tasks should contain little structure and require low supervision. (T1, T7, T14, T12, T8)
24. Job should consist of a variety of tasks. (T12, T10, T13)
25. Task should contain minimal financial or technical component. (T20, T2)
26. Task should be of central importance to the organization. (T2, T19)
27. Task should consist of large amounts of new learning and use of MBA skills and provide people-intensive opportunities. (T6, T5)
28. Task should permit high degree of creativity. (T7, T21)
29. Task should have a measurable outcome. (T2, T10, T25)
30. Task should be ambiguous, but lend itself to being organized. (T20)

have followed the outline, you have been using inductive logic to build from specific data a list of general Life Themes and Implications, and inductive thinking is hard work. Go home. Let the papers sit for a while, and then go on to Step 9.

Step 9: Life Themes According to Friends

Take your list of Life Themes and show it to people who you feel know you well—spouse, close friends, other family members, roommates, people who have seen you in a variety of settings. Ask them to read the list and make notes or comments about what they see. Ask them to make additions where they think you have left something out.

Be very careful not to try to convince people about the validity of the items on your list or to persuade them to change their suggestions about adding to it or subtracting from it. You may not agree with what they say, but for the sake of getting their honest opinion, try not to be defensive. Do not argue against whatever suggestions they may make. Once you have written down the suggestions and ideas from three or four people, sit down again with your list of themes and make the changes that you feel are appropriate or accurate. Then make any changes in your implications suggested by the Life Theme revisions.

Once your list of Implications is complete, put it in your notebook.

Your list of Implications provides criteria for considering job opportunities and for making job-related decisions. The list will help you to be more focused, more effective, and more efficient in your job search activities.

Step 10: Criteria Checklist

At this point you can develop a "Criteria Checklist" from your lists of Life Themes and Implications. The checklist is a one-page sheet with phrases that remind you of the criteria you have developed in your self-assessment exercise; see the example in Figure 1-7.

Figure   1-7

JEWEL SAVADELIS'S CRITERIA CHECKLIST

From Themes

1. Gives opportunity to control.
2. Gives opportunity to deal with people.
3. Involves significant ends.
4. Gives opportunity to improve self.
5. Allows creativity.
6. Includes some risk.
7. Company is good at giving praise and recognition.
8. Company allows new people to be effective.
9. Company respects new people.
10. Has flexible schedule.
11. Offers good compensation.
12. Is near friends and family.
13. Has no marathon projects.
14. Treats women equally.
15. Permits organization.
16. Requires intuitive thinking.
17. Is not conventional.
18. Company moves quickly.
19. Company has a practical orientation.

From Implications

20. Is a renegade company.
21. Allows time for outside activities.
22. Company encourages personal growth.
23. Offers open access to all levels.
24. Are fair and ethical leaders.
25. Company values employees.
26. Provides pleasant surroundings.
27. Manufactures for-profit tangible product.
28. Permits time for self.
29. Permits time for family.
30. Permits time for social activities.
31. Has attractive location.
32. Colleagues are diverse.
33. Boss is nonauthoritarian.
34. Peers are nonrigid, bright, unconventional.

35. Has open, informal atmosphere.
36. Employees treated with respect, honesty, and encouragement.
37. Includes ambiguous authority structure.
38. Provides leadership opportunities.
39. Team members are willing to carry their share.
40. Has little structure and low supervision.
41. Offers a variety of tasks.
42. Has minimal financial and technical components.
43. Has central importance to company.
44. Requires new learning, use MBA skills.
45. Provides measurable outcome.
46. Offers ambiguous but organizable task.

Keep this checklist beside your telephone or in your appointment book. The criteria are a screen for deciding whether or not you want to spend the considerable time and effort it takes to follow up on an opportunity. You may get telephone calls saying, "Come to Houston (or Denver or Seattle). We want you to consider working for us." Before you decide to go to the expense in money, time, and energy to research the company and to make the trip, you can ask some specific questions, drawn directly from your list of Implications, about the characteristics of the job. You might ask about involvement with people, autonomy in the job, travel, or whatever it is that you have on your checklist.

Whenever you go on a job search, keep the checklist handy.

Remember, it is not just the companies who are doing the screening; *you* also are screening them. A productive job decision is one that matches individual characteristics with organizational needs. If either side in that contract makes an inappropriate decision, the outcome is likely to be unhappy for both sides. So it is as much your responsibility as it is the company's to gather the kind of information necessary to make a good match.

Recruiters vary in their interviewing skills. Some are not able to ask the right questions or to volunteer appropriate data on the job or company. Since you share with the recruiters the responsibility for a good decision, you have to manage not only giving information but also collecting information. Your checklist of Implications will help you to do that by reminding you of the kinds of data that you need to collect—data related directly to your Life Themes. Do not show the checklist to recruiters or tell them that you have gone through this exercise; rather, just use the self-knowledge to ask the right questions so that you can get the information you need.

CONCLUSION

The process we have outlined involves a relatively quick and multifaceted self-assessment that will help you to develop a focus for your job search activities, for your recruiting activities, and for your career decision making. It does not necessarily give you a 100 percent accurate outline of the characteristics that you should be considering, but if you have been careful as you have gone along and have pressed yourself to be honest, it will be more accurate than not.

The approach we have taken is intended to have you look at a variety of dimensions about yourself in the belief that no single aspect can give you the kind of information you need to make a career decision. By looking at a variety of dimensions, you can begin to develop themes, patterns, or trends that are more likely to be an accurate description of who you are and who you are becoming than would a simple analysis of, say, your economic goals alone.

If this process has led you to feel the need to explore some areas more carefully or to use some professional help in developing some further information about yourself, seek other sources and spend some additional time on your self-assessment activities. You may, for instance, want to buy the book, *Self-Assessment and Career Development*, which offers a much more extended program of activities for self-assessment than has been possible in this chapter. Or you may wish to contact a career counselor—there are many counselors in private practice and many associated with universities or other institutions. Before you make a commitment to any of these counselors, however, do some homework to discover their reputations and the results of their work (by asking them what their services are, and what the credentials and training of their counselors are, and by talking to people who have used them before), so that you can assess the accuracy and the validity of the advice that they may give you. Remember, there is no crystal ball; there are no magic answers. Developing a set of self-assessment data that will be a benefit to you is a matter of hard work, honesty, and careful interpretation.

2 CAREER CONCEPTS

Now that you have developed a relatively detailed self-assessment, we encourage you to consider the *type* of career you wish to have before deciding what industry or functional specialty to choose for your first post-MBA job. The first job you accept, even if it is a short-term position, can have a profound effect on the pattern or shape of your career. Many MBAs are directed informally, through peer pressure and their business school placement offices, to accept highly structured positions with *Fortune 500* firms. "Success" is then simply assumed to mean accumulating the greatest possible amount of responsibility, power, and money over the shortest possible time, as shown in Figure 2-1(a). This type of career path may indeed meet the desires and needs of many MBAs. Others, however, may prefer to perfect a particular skill or to increase their expertise and knowledge in a particular area throughout their career; for them, a "successful" career path is horizontal rather than vertical, as shown in Figure 2-1(b). Still others may prefer a career in which they can develop many talents, at once or sequentially, as shown in Figure 2-1(c). And some may choose activities other than work as the central object of their efforts. These people tend to hop from job to job, in the transitory pattern shown in Figure 2-1(d).

Consider these comments by Professor Mike Driver of the University of Southern California, who first identified these naturally occurring patterns:

> Each person has some concept in mind when the term career is used, but in some cases the concept is very simple or confused, and in others, it may be a very elaborate, long-range plan embracing not only one's job but one's family and hobbies as well.[1]
>
> Certain strange-appearing career patterns may be understood only by examining nonwork factors—for example, a "happily" adapted person in a "dead-end" job may in fact see his career as centered on a key hobby, such as Boy Scout leader or on his family.[2]

Professor Driver has devised a theory of career concepts for looking at different, naturally occurring career patterns and their effects on the individual. Driver's theory suggests that different cognitive styles, decision-making processes, and career motives determine the career concept that an individual will implement in his or her life. Driver outlines four basic career concepts:

> The *Linear* career concept embodies the notion that a career is a series of upward moves within a field. There may be changes in organization to avoid blocking but the key ingredient is steady upward movement—particularly in an organizational sense.[3]
>
> A critical factor separating this pattern from the Steady State is its nearly insatiable upward pattern. Hobbies and family may often be "orchestrated" to support this upward surge (which may result in neglect of real family needs).[4]
>
> The *Steady State* concept refers to a view of career in which one makes an early commitment to a field and holds to it for life. There may be minor changes (i.e., of organization) and some inner growth of competence in one's field leading to some up-

Figure 2-1

DRIVER'S CAREER CONCEPTS

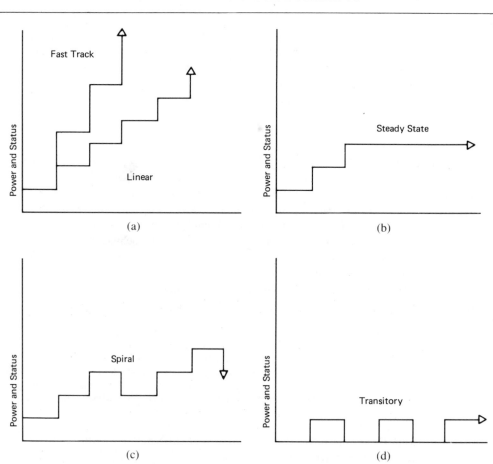

ward movement, but the essential thing is a fixed identity within the field. This concept may be associated with professions or skilled trades.[5]

MBAs who might follow this pattern are investment managers and consultants. As with Transitory people, Steady-Staters can be found in both active and passive roles: (1) the passive (at work) security seeker who invests energy in nonwork-related activities or who fears failure; and (2) the active professional who strives to attain and then maintain a level of expertise.[6,7]

The *Spiral* path is so named because it seems a non-random pattern of career change, often apparently lateral (from a Linear view), possibly even downward. Yet there does seem to be an inner pattern of self-growth that I feel can be symbolized by a Spiral leading outward towards ever-widening self-awareness. The movements on this path seem oddly cyclic (5–7 years), although the intervals may decrease as one goes through successive changes. Movement in this career path usually involves integration of family, hobbies, and work.[8]

Perhaps a useful subdivision of Spiral patterns is: (1) an Internal Spiral—who stays within an organization or professional field, yet moves around creatively in search of self-development; and (2) an External Spiral—who more dramatically switches organizations and fields in the same search.[9]

The *Transitory* concept describes a career pattern with no apparent direction. Individuals following such a pattern make frequent and major changes in jobs and industries. These are most often lateral rather than upward moves. Driver indicates that two types of Transitories can be found: (1) "an independent, non-entrepreneurial, relatively passive type who drifts from job to job—whose major need is freedom to move on"; and (2) "an entrepreneurial active type who keeps innovating new activities, yet gets out as soon as stabilization sets in."[9] It is common to find Transitories whose job is only a means of supporting some other activity, such as a sport or hobby on the positive side or an addiction on the negative side.

The Linear career concept is the one most often associated with MBAs. Examples of this concept include those who enter any functional area of a corporation and work upward to positions of increasing responsibility.

Driver also notes, "Each Career Concept has its own unique problems as well as advantages." For instance, the Transitory, although "free and enterprising," may suffer from "identity confusion." The Steady-State person may be full of pride of place, or quietly and desperately suffering from lack of growth and development. The Linear pattern can lead to immense success but also to a great variety of crises, such as plateauing, being advanced beyond the limits of competence, neglecting of the total self, alienation from family, and so on. Spirals perhaps have the greatest self-fulfillment but possibily also the worst woes. "Being mistaken for failures or classed as 'crazy' is among their headaches."[10]

There are questions as to whether career concepts are static or dynamic (i.e., once a Linear always a Linear?). It seems logical, however, that since both work and nonwork factors can change, so also can the motivations that nudge us toward implementing a particular career pattern in our lives.

We have included portions of Driver's work here because we believe that MBAs should be aware of alternative career concepts, and not just the Linear mold in which they are often placed. Each concept has its rewards and drawbacks, which depend upon one's own career motivations. Yet organization career paths and reward systems often recognize only the Linear types, thus encouraging those who may not be Linear, or may not want to be, to fit into the Linear pattern.

One of the significant implications of Driver's research is that it legitimizes alternative career concepts. Organizations *need* all four types to succeed—the Linear to manage, the Steady State to know the details and to do the bread-and-butter jobs, the Spiral to innovate, and the Transitory to respond to business cycles. Driver's work also asks managers to consider carefully how they can develop pluralistic reward systems that recognize the value of each type to the firm. You need to identify a career concept based on your needs and then seek employers and job opportunities where this approach will be appreciated and rewarded. This advance preparation can help you to avoid career successes that result in personal failures and help ensure career decisions that serve career and personal goals alike.

NOTES

1. Mike Driver, "Career Concepts and Career Management in Organizations," in Cary Cooper, ed., *Behavioral Problems in Organizations*, (Englewood Cliffs, N.J.: Prentice-Hall, 1978), p. 85.
2. Ibid., p. 84.
3. Ibid., p. 87.
4. Ibid., p. 92.
5. Driver, "Career Concepts and Organizational Development," p. 7, paper presented at the Academy of Management Annual Meeting, San Francisco, August 1978.
6. Op. cit., p. 102.
7. Driver refers to two works by E. Schein on career anchors, or motives, that determine the career paths chosen by individuals: see E. Schein, "Career Anchors and Career Paths: A Panel Study of Management School Graduates," in J. Van Maanen, ed., *Organizational Career: Some New Perspectives* (London: Wiley-Interscience, 1977). Also see E. Schein, *The Individual, the Organization and the Career* (Reading, Mass.: Addison-Wesley, 1968).
8. Driver, "Career Concepts and Career Management in Organizations," p. 92.
9. Ibid., p. 93.
10. Ibid., p. 95.

3   THE JOB RESEARCH REPORT GRID

To simplify further and speed the process of using your personal data to manage and direct your career, we have developed the Job Research Report Grid which you can use to match a job's qualifications with your own. We believe that individuals and jobs can *both* be described by certain characteristics or dimensions and that having assessments on both sides is essential to developing a fit. We have selected ten dimensions that we think you should assess both in yourself and in your job opportunities. These are:

Education
Experience
Location
Compensation
Work involvement
Pace
Career path
Interpersonal style
Cognitive style
Variety

These dimensions apply to individuals and career fields in a general way: the specifics (e.g., of education) may vary from job to job, but the approximate degree to which the ratings—yours and the job's—overlap on each dimension can help you to fit your self-assessment to a job opportunity.

As we have said, assessing the dimensions of poor fit as you look for and decide upon a job is as important as assessing the dimensions of good fit. If you take a job that you don't fit on two or three dimensions and you are aware of that, you can begin to lay plans for how you are going to manage the misfits and thus reduce your career vulnerability in those areas.

We encourage you to use your self-assessment themes and implications to complete the Personal Job Search Profile card (see page 22). Note that these are "level" ratings more than "topical" ratings. Thus, although a master's degree in chemistry may match the "level" requirement for a job in management, the topical area is inappropriate. We leave it to you to assess the topical relevance of your education to the job opportunity.

Use a sharp pencil to punch out your self-rating on each dimension. Use care in building from your self-assessment so that the Personal Profile card is based on accurate data and not on a momentary whim.

The Job Research Report Grids at the beginning of each of the following chapters are designed to provide information at a glance about the ten dimensions for that job. By placing your grid over the grid that introduces each chapter, you will be able to see quickly how compatible you are *generally* with a particular position. If it ap-

Personal Job Search Profile Card

for _____   (Date: /   /   )

Education (degrees)	BA	MBA	PhD
Experience required (yrs)	None	1-3	3+
Location	Urban	Rural	Regional / Travel
Compensation ($/yr)	< $25K	$25-30K	$30-35K / >$35K
Work involvement (hrs/wk)	< 50	50-60	> 60
Pace	Relaxed	Medium	Frenetic
Career path (a la Driver)	Spiral	Steady	Linear
Interpersonal style	Loner	Moderate	Outgoing
Cognitive style	Sequential Rules Details	Mixed Principles Systems	Random Free form Big picture
Variety (preference for)	No change Ordered	Occasional change	Ambiguous Changing

pears that there is a high degree of fit with that job, you may wish to read the description in greater detail. If not, you might skip it and go on to the next one.

The grids are intended to provide a digest of the information contained in the Job Research Reports. The simplified format has necessarily led to some generalizations. Use the grid, therefore, as a *general* introduction to those reports that are of interest or that match your personal Themes and Implications, but do not use them as an authority as to whether or not you should pursue a particular job opportunity.

Notes on the Rating of Each Dimension

Many of the dimensions are rated on a high-medium-low basis. We have used the following guidelines for rating each job criterion and suggest that you use corresponding definitions as you develop your own profile.

1. *Education*. This section is rated either a PhD or an MBA from one of the top-tier business schools,* an MBA degree in general is needed, and a BA. These are general educational requirements; "MBA," for example, means that someone with a lower educational background may be hired, but less frequently.

2. *Experience*. Here we indicate whether three or more years of job-related experience, one to three years, or no experience is necessary for the job.

3. *Location*. This criterion describes the geographical environment of the position. "Urban" and "Rural" are self-explanatory. "Regional" means focused in a particular part of the country. "Travel" means that the job requires frequent movement and has no real base location.

4. *Compensation*. The figures are self-explanatory and match the four brackets on the Personal Profile card. Note that these salaries, given also in the Job Research Reports, reflect the salaries of top-tier business school students in 1983-1984. "K" refers to "thousands."

5. *Work involvement*. This criterion estimates the number of hours needed on average to do well in the job: 60 or more hours per week, 50 to 60 hours, and 40 to 50 hours per week.

6. *Pace*. This criterion refers to the intensity of the work as opposed to the number of hours required. The high-medium-low ratings are our estimates of the job pace.

7. *Career path*. Linear, Spiral, and Steady State are defined in the chapter on career concepts. Transitory has not been included because it is less relevant to MBAs.

8. *Interpersonal style*. This dimension seeks to rate the amount of social contact demanded by a job. We have assumed that outgoing people tend to be more assertive in their behavior.

9. *Cognitive style*. This criterion describes a mode of thinking or analyzing. "Sequential, Rules, Details" refers to jobs filled by people who prefer to think within a defined structure, in step-by-step fashion, and with attention to details. "Random, Free form, Big picture" refers to jobs peopled by those who prefer no set order in their thinking, who typically muddle around until they sense the "gestalt" of the larger problem, and who therefore are more individualistic in their thinking. In between, "Mixed, Principles, and Systems" refers to jobs that de-

---

*Degrees from certain nationally known and ranked schools generally command greater salaries and opportunities. This list usually includes Harvard, Stanford, Chicago, Wharton, Columbia, Dartmouth, Virginia, Berkeley, Northwestern, Indiana, and UCLA.

mand both sequential and random analysis, or that focus on midlevel systems and principles.

10. *Variety*. These ratings refer to variety in job structure. Thus, the job of telephone soliciting all day long would be on the "No change, Ordered" end of the spectrum because even though there may be variation in how the people on the other end respond, the task itself (dialing and repeating a set sales pitch and noting responses) is repetitive.

4 WRITING COVER LETTERS

Cover letters go with a resume as your introduction to the firm. As does the resume, cover letters provide limited contact with the recruiter, so it is important that the impression left is the one you want. That does not mean that you should try to leave a favorable impression with every reader—even in the same industry, organizations vary widely in their culture and therefore in their fit to you as an individual. Your letter should communicate clearly who you are, what your objective is, what you have to offer, what you are looking for, and who will take the next step.

First, you have to know to whom to send the letter. One person we know found some addresses in an industry directory and sent off a barrage of letters. Most of them were returned with notes like, "We are sorry. So-and-so passed away two years ago," or "So-and-so does not work for us anymore." If you cannot get a direct reference from a contact (faculty, friend, or alumnus), call the firm, tell the receptionist who you are, and find out who is the line manager in charge of the function you're seeking to fill. If you do not have a specific functional area in mind, but are more interested in the company or general management, inquire about the general manager of the division or region in which you are interested.

We recommend that you go first to the line manager. If you are of interest to the firm, the manager will either contact you directly or refer your application to the personnel manager. If you send your resume directly to the personnel manager, your application will be dealt with in a much more routine fashion, since the personnel department may process hundreds of applications a day during peak periods. Furthermore, the personnel department is a screening function. The final decision is usually made by the line managers or at least on their recommendation. If you start there, and get their support, you are more likely to get past the personnel screen.

Having confirmed the proper destination for your letter, you must write it. The first paragraph should say who you are and why you are writing. You are writing because you are seeking the kind of employment that will fit who you are and because your initial research on the firm indicates that the opportunities that the company faces, and its approach to meeting those challenges, are similar to your own. In other words, you want to communicate that this is not just another shotgun letter, but the result of a careful self-assessment (like the one you did in your weekend exercise) and a careful company and industry assessment (like the one you will have to do when you write this letter).

The second paragraph should outline what you are looking for in terms of the challenges that face the company. Read about the firm; look up newspaper articles and magazine articles to get a sense of its recent history and the conditions it faces in its major markets. Then, using your school-developed skills of analysis, anticipate the major challenges that face the firm and note them as the kinds of problems you seek to encounter in your career. Describe the kind of firm that you want to work for—something about its culture as well as its business opportunities. This will turn off companies that are not like the ones you describe, but will turn on companies that are. You would rather know that in advance anyway.

The third paragraph should describe what you have to offer as a resource for meeting the challenges and opportunities outlined in the second paragraph. Refer to your attached resume, but do not repeat information contained in it. Outline the personal skills and attributes that may not emerge from the resume's formal structure. The trick here is be descriptive but not to appear arrogant or difficult to work with.

The last paragraph should outline clearly what the next step is. It is much easier to read a cover letter and a resume and throw it in the wastebasket than it is to say "No!" on the telephone. The more personal your contact with the recruiter, the more likely you both are to have accurate information about each other and to establish a relationship. Consequently, you should say that you will telephone the individual in the next week to discuss the letter and their reaction to it. This way, you will know what the outcome is and will not be left hanging. If like most letters yours merely asks for a response, and you don't hear anything, you don't know if the letter was lost in the mail, forwarded to another department, thrown away, or put on the fast track. By keeping the ball in your court, you control the next contact time.

When you call, you can introduce yourself and note that you sent a letter and resume last week. If it was not received, you can explain what you wrote in the letter and offer to send another. If it was received, you can ask the manager's reaction to it. If the answer is a clear "No," use the moment to gather some additional information. You might ask, "Thank you for your time. Before we hang up, I would like to ask one additional question. Given the research I did on your company and my knowledge of who I am and what I can do, I felt there was a good fit. What was it that led you to conclude otherwise?" The answer to this question will give you some information about your letter, your resume, your analysis, or the state of the company's hiring activities. That information can go a long way toward reassuring you emotionally, helping you improve your letter and resume, and understanding the firm.

The letter in Figure 4-1 uses the approach we have outlined here. This particular letter was the result of hours of research and twenty-five drafts. The individual knew just what he wanted and enough about the twelve companies to which he sent the letter to compare what he wanted with what they needed and offered. Some companies were put off by his letter, but most were enthusiastic in their response. He got 10 callbacks.

When you have drafted your cover letters (one for each firm), ask a friend to read and critique them. Remember that your friend's feedback may not fit the approach you are taking, but use that information as a check on your style.

Figure   4.1

A SAMPLE COVER LETTER

Dear Mr. _____ :

    I shall receive an M.B.A. in June 1978, and plan a career in the real estate field with a leading properties firm. My survey of the industry indicates that your firm has established an outstanding record and, therefore, it would be advantageous for me to learn more about the specific opportunities it offers and to discuss with you my objectives and capabilities.

    My highest priority is to find a challenging, fulfilling environment in which to learn and work. Pursuant to this objective, I seek a firm which: (1) recognizes the need for professional management of M.B.A. caliber in this rapidly growing field, (2) gives a broad exposure to real estate and discourages overspecialization, (3) operates in an informal structure with close personal relationships among employees, (4) allows new M.B.A.'s to contribute immediately and to assume early responsibilities, and (5) measures performance without regard for seniority. I would like to know more about your firm with respect to these criteria.

    The enclosed resume gives you a brief outline of my background but does not deal with relevant personal qualities. I have an entrepreneurial spirit, the ability to coordinate several projects simultaneously with proven results, and a "knack" for working successfully with diverse groups of people eliciting their trust and confidence. I am performance-oriented, mature, willing to travel, able to communicate effectively, and confident that the pattern of success that has characterized my past will lead me to greater achievements in the near future.

    Mr. _____ , if you feel that my objectives and qualifications may be compatible with your firm's opportunities and needs, please contact me to arrange a meeting that could be to our mutual benefit. I shall hope to hear from you soon.

                          Sincerely,

                          James L. Lydon

JLL/lmm
enclosure

---

5 WRITING EFFECTIVE RESUMES

Resumes are like short stories. Every word, every phrase, every fact—even the format of the print on the page—leaves an impression in the reader's mind. As the most important document introducing you to the recruiter, the resume communicates, like a short story, a feeling as well as cognitive information. That feeling and the facts will go together to form an impression of the candidate—positive, neutral, or negative. Resumes that are seen as neutral or negative will probably be put aside in favor of the positive ones. Thus, those who can write an effective resume, like those who can write an effective short story, will find their work being read again.

Resume readers may look through 100 resumes in a day. Reading so many, they develop a rhythm and a routine, quickly screening out the worst, saving the best for review. As they read, anything that stands out will capture their attention. Sometimes the things that break their rhythmic reading will cast a favorable light on the author; other times the interruption is a jarring one that signals a misfit between the opening and the candidate.

Recruiters look for relevant technical experience and for professionalism—but they also get an impression that tells them whether or not the author of this particular resume deserves greater attention. You, the resume writer, must remember to control the impression as well as the facts that your resume gives the recruiter. If you hope to get beyond the initial screening, your resume must leave the reader with confidence and curiosity—confidence that the background and experience is relevant to the company and curiosity to know more about the interesting person who wrote the resume. To create these reactions to your resume, you must, like the short-story author, pay careful attention to every detail. Every decision about what to put in, how to word it, how to lay it out on the page will contribute to that final impression. You must be aware of these decisions and control as well as you can the conclusion that will be drawn by those who read your resume. Make sure that *everything* you put in your resume, including each formatting decision, has an explicit and particular purpose in your mind.

Format

The first thing a recruiter sees when he or she picks up your resume is the format of the print on the page. That leaves a visual impression of the individual who wrote it. We remember that two of the sixty graduating MBAs at my alma mater had a professional firm lay out their resumes. It cost a little more, but when interviewing, they both were told that the appearance of their resume said to the readers, "This person is a professional. Outstanding."

The format of your resume should be chosen with several criteria in mind. First, it should highlight the important features of your resume, namely what, where, and when—and in that order. Resumes, like the one in Figure 5-2, that highlight the dates by putting them on the visually central line of each entry, understate the what and the where of the person's experience. It is much more important to know what a person did and with what firm than to know when.

Second, your format should be visually simple and easy to read. Narrow margins and complex paragraphing schemes make the resume look busy and cluttered—not the kind of initial impression you would like to leave.

Third, your format should be consistent. Remember that anything you do on your resume that breaks the readers' rhythm or causes them to pause and take note should be something you intended—something that creates the impression you wanted it to make. Unfortunately, the most common rhythm breakers are jarring factors like poor grammar, misspellings, and inconsistent format. These all leave negative impressions.

One common inconsistency is to begin each entry paragraph with a different part of speech. If the reader gets a noun at the beginning of the first paragraph, he or she should get a noun at the beginning of each paragraph. Subconsciously, that is what one expects and to encounter suddenly an initial verb two paragraphs down forces the reader to stop and reorganize the information being taken in. To do this more than once is confusing; to do it just once is more confusing than you can afford to be. Thus, you should begin every paragraph with the *title* (a noun) that you held. Under "Education," therefore, the first word will often be "Graduate." Under "Experience" you can say "Assistant Vice-President" or whatever other title you may have held, and so on.

We have included copies of poorly written and well-written resumes to contrast. We like the format presented in Figure 5-4 because it highlights the what, the where, and the when immediately and leaves plenty of room for relatively detailed descriptions of the "how" beneath each heading. Notice that each entry begins with the company and place on the key line and the *name* of the job as the first word in the explanatory paragraph. Each clause that follows the name begins with an action verb that describes what the person did in that setting. Many writers of resumes have listed appropriate action verbs. A list of some common useful ones appears in Figure 5-1.

Figure 5-1

SOME USEFUL ACTION VERBS	
organized	collected
built	raised
managed	opened
analyzed	established
conducted	incorporated
hired	created
selected	wrote
presented	increased

Professional Objectives

We do not believe that professional objectives are useful on a resume. They limit the flexibility and usefulness of the resume in a variety of recruiting situations and are best left for the cover letter.

Many major business schools publish and distribute resume books.* In this situation, where the resume is the only document that a recruiter may have to review your qualifications, professional objectives may have to be included. Even in that case, we recommend omitting a professional objective and sending a cover letter with resume to the corporations you wish to contact on the mailing list of your business school. The argument for including them says that one should provide some area of focus in a way that does not limit one's options unnecessarily. In our experience, people who try to do this often lose more than they gain because their attempts to "maintain their options" create an objective that is so unclear as to be useless. This leaves an impression of vagueness and indecision. To have no professional objective on the resume itself allows recruiters to draw their own conclusions about whether or not the candidate's background fits their openings. Some will argue that the recruiter will not take the time to read, in a resume book, a resume that has no objective, but this goes against common sense. If the format is such that the relevant experience stands out, the reader's attention will be captured.

If you wish to leave a professional objective on your resume, focus it toward a particular career alternative. Some people who put their resumes in resume books never get any calls. In some cases this is because their professional objectives are so diffuse that no recruiter can read them and say "This person is a good fit for what we want." So although resume books are generally used for a "flock shooting" approach, you should use them as a "rifle shot" if you include a professional objective. You will get more responses. All of this will make more sense when you realize that in a typical year, less than 10 percent of the job offers finally accepted by graduates of a well-known Eastern business school come through the resume book and that people who are reading resume books are skimming hundreds of resumes and are likely to take the ones that have focus over those that don't, all things being equal.

As an example, consider the objective in Figure 5-2. The "objective" is so broad that the reader is left wondering what the person really wants—and concluding that the person does not really know. If you must include a professional objective, make it specific.

Educational Experience

Most people list under educational experience only the school, their degree, and any academic honors they may have won, but there is much more that is relevant to the resume and to managing the impression you give the resume

---

*Some schools collect the resumes of all of their graduating students, bind them into a single volume with an index of names categorized by job interest, and distribute or sell them to major corporate recruiters.

Figure 5-2

JOHNNIE B. SINGER
Route 6, Box 27A
Hampton, Pennsylvania 88301

Box 4320
University of South Virginia
Shelley, Virginia 22909

EMPLOYMENT
OBJECTIVE
A position in marketing, finance, or operations that will give me training in becoming a general manager.

EDUCATION
September 1980 to Present

University of South Virginia, MBA, Shelley, Virginia.
Operations Club, International Business Club, Finance Club, Marketing Club, Consulting Club.

September 1974 to May 1978

Dayton University, Dayton, Missouri, BA Accounting, FILLMORE AWARD, President Psi Beta Sigma, NROTC.

EXPERIENCE
Summer 1980

Tiny Toys, Inc., Phoenix, Arizona
Market Analyst assigned to Southern California. Examined the product potential for a new product to be introduced in L.A.

August 1978 to August 1980

Tonka Toys, Inc., New York, New York
Prepared production plans for major plant as a planning analyst. Assisted with negotiations with suppliers. Duties included buying managing and inventory.

May 1977 to June 1978

Assistant to the President, Dayton University. Wrote speeches, briefed for appointments, general administration.

PERSONAL
Date of birth: 2/15/56.
Interests: tennis, cooking, photography, movies.
Languages: German.
Skills: typing.
Also like traveling and sailing.

REFERENCES
Mr. John Drew
President, Dayton University
P.O. Box 5990
Dayton, Missouri 43708

JOHNNIE B. SINGER   *where is he?*
Route 6, Box 27A
Hampton, Pennsylvania 88301   Box 4320
University of South Virginia
Shelley, Virginia 22909

TELEPHONE?

giving or getting   *which?*   *giving or getting*

EMPLOYMENT OBJECTIVE   A position in marketing, finance, or operations that will give me training in becoming a general manager.

EDUCATION   September 1980 to Present

DO MORE THAN PAY dUES?   University of South Virginia, MBA, Shelley, Virginia. Operations Club, International Business Club, Finance Club, Marketing Club, Consulting Club.

September 1974 to May 1978   *Date should not be main focus.*

FOR WHAT?   Dayton University, Dayton, Missouri, BA Accounting, FILLMORE AWARD, President Psi Beta Sigma, NROTC.

EXPERIENCE   Summer 1980   *DID WHAT?*

WASTED LINES   Tiny Toys, Inc., Phoenix, Arizona
Market Analyst assigned to Southern California. Examined the product potential for a new product to be introduced in L.A.

August 1978 to August 1980

Tonka Toys, Inc., New York, New York
Prepared production plans for major plant as a planning analyst.
INCONSISTANT FORMAT   Assisted with negotiations with suppliers. Duties included buying managing and inventory.

May 1977 to June 1978

Assistant to the President, Dayton University. Wrote speeches, briefed for appointments, general administration.   *what's this?*

PERSONAL   Date of birth: 2/15/56.
Interests: tennis, cooking, sports, photography, movies.
Languages: German.
Skills: typing.
Also like traveling and sailing.   *plays a lot*

REFERENCES   Mr. John Drew
President, Dayton University   *NAMEdROPPER?*
P.O. Box 5990
Dayton, Missouri 43708

Figure 5-4

DAVID R. BOYLE

13-B9 Marion Hill   Home Telephone: 808-974-8923
Shelley, Virginia 88402   Office Telephone: 603-234-3454

EDUCATION 1982-1984	UNIVERSITY OF SOUTHERN VIRGINIA Shelley, Virginia Candidate, MBA; awarded Calhoun Award for Academic Excellence by select faculty panel; President, Marketing Club, responsible for increasing membership, responding to student needs, inviting speakers; organized basketball league in response to student demands.
1974–1978	MAPLETON COLLEGE Mapleton, New Jersey Graduate, B.A. economics; Dean's List; President, Psi Kappa Sigma Fraternity, responsible for recruiting new members, maintaining high academic standards, researching campus needs, organizing community service drives, and maintaining close relationships with school administration; varsity tennis, elected Captain, 1978.
EXPERIENCE 1980-1982	SOUTHERN METALS CORPORATION Atlanta, Georgia Production Analyst; researched and analyzed production flows for 600,000-ton/month process, coordinated with marketing to ensure responsiveness to market pressures, developed break-even analysis for each of 57 products, prepared detailed report, presented it to senior management, of recommendations now being implemented by the firm, designed and programmed a computer system to update these data regularly, supervised three other analysts.
1978–1980	GREEN CROSS HOSPITAL Green Cross, Georgia Assistant Director of Community Relations; built and maintained close relationships with community to make sure the hospital responded to community needs, analyzed hospital service usage in comparison with public needs, recommended changes to Administrator, later accepted.
PERSONAL	I have a great interest in understanding consumer behavior, which supports my profesional ambition. I am also an experienced computer user.
REFERENCES	Available upon request.

---

reader. Any activity, whether it is related to church, fraternity, sorority, or social events—any outside or extracurricular activities that involve experience that is in any way related to the job opportunities you are seeking—is appropriate to mention.

When the reader has finished reading your resume, he or she should have a

Figure 5-5

DAVID R. BOYLE

13-B9 Marion Hill   Home Telephone: 808-974-8923
Shelley, Virginia 88402   Office Telephone: 603-234-3454

EDUCATION 1982-1984	UNIVERSITY OF SOUTHERN VIRGINIA Shelley, Virginia Candidate, MBA; awarded Calhoun Award for Academic Excellence by select faculty panel; President, Marketing Club, responsible for increasing membership, responding to student needs, inviting speakers; organized basketball league in response to student demands.
1974–1978	MAPLETON COLLEGE Mapleton, New Jersey Graduate, B.A. economics; Dean's List; President, Psi Kappa Sigma Fraternity, responsible for recruiting new members, maintaining high academic standards, researching campus needs, organizing community service drives, and maintaining close relationships with school administration; varsity tennis, elected Captain, 1978.
EXPERIENCE	SOUTHERN METALS CORPORATION Atlanta, Georgia Production Analyst; researched and analyzed production flows for 600,000-ton/month process, coordinated with marketing to ensure responsiveness to market pressures, developed break-even analysis for each of 57 products, prepared detailed report, presented it to senior management, of recommendations now being implemented by the firm, designed and programmed a computer system to update these data regularly, supervised three other analysts.
1978–1980	GREEN CROSS HOSPITAL Green Cross, Georgia Assistant Director of Community Relations; built and maintained close relationships with community to make sure the hospital responded to community needs, analyzed hospital service usage in comparison with public needs, recommended changes to Administrator, later accepted.
PERSONAL	I have a great interest in understanding consumer behavior, which supports my profesional ambition. I am also an experienced computer user.

CONSISTENT
MARKETING RESEARCH
THEME

REFERENCES   Available upon request.

SUBTHEMES: Management, Computers

---

clear-cut theme in mind, a pattern of skill and experience development that relates
directly to the job at hand. Although the reader may not actually circle and
connect the elements that form the theme, as we have done in Figures 5-3 and 5-
5, the impression will either be there or not be there in the reader's mind. For
instance, if you are looking for a job in marketing research, you should scrutinize
all your past experiences for activities that taught you anything about marketing

research. Activities in which you surveyed, analyzed, sampled, worked with end users or consumers, and so on should be noted with the appropriate words.

If you were seeking a job in commercial banking and were the treasurer of your fraternity or the fund manager for the campus play or did anything else that involved the handling of money or the coordinating of financial services with individuals, you should note this on your resume under the name of the academic institution at which you received your education. Every word will leave an impression in the recruiter's mind at a conscious or subconscious level. If, by the time one gets to the bottom of your resume, he or she has read financially related words like "budgeted," "calculated," "interest," "income," "profits," the reader is likely to have a much stronger impression that you fit the opportunity.

Experience

Under this heading you include all your related work and noneducational experience. As you did under the "Education" section, review carefully everything you have done, looking for the activities that gave you some relevant experience and training. This does not mean that you exaggerate your experience—most people tend to err in the other direction anyway, ignoring activities that gave them relevant experience—rather, it asks you to highlight the aspects of your background that are related to the job. Again, use action verbs that are directly related to the career opportunity that you are seeking.

Personal References and Data

We recommend omitting any specifics with regard to personal references, hobbies, and other personal data unless they add to a particular impression that you desire to make. We have seen resumes, for instance, where the individual was applying for a job in construction and listed under personal references that he liked "cooking." Now there is nothing wrong with cooking, and this person may well have been a good cook, but the impression created is not one that fits most of the people in the construction industry. Try to imagine the mind set and the perspective of the resume reader and create the kind of impression that will get you past the first screen.

Summary

Good resumes leave the reader with the kind of impression that the writer desires. They are targeted to a specific occupational objective and communicate it with recurring development of a theme throughout the resume. Effective resumes manage the impression that the recruiter gets by carefully laying out a consistent format, by highlighting activities that relate to the opening, and by omitting data that do not relate to the job at hand.

Part 2

JOB RESEARCH REPORTS

INTRODUCTION

The remainder of this book incorporates data gathered by MBA students on various industries and job opportunities that utilize MBA skills. Although every effort has been made to ensure the accuracy of this information, it is important to note that it is based on the perceptions of these students, formed through research, interviews with alumni, and so on. The research was performed by students from the Harvard and University of Virginia business schools, and their bias should be noted.

Each job report is divided into the following sections, in order:

Title: the name of the function or industry reported.

Grid: the Job Research Report Grid marked differently for each industry. We encourage you to complete your own grid profile (see Section 4), punch out the perforated rectangles that match your characteristics, tear it out of the book, and then compare it with the grid for jobs you find interesting. A good match would be indicated by a solid shaded profile showing through; a poor match would be all white. (Note that on some reports, dimensions of the grid are marked at several levels: we did this to indicate that people with different characteristics on that dimension might well fit that job.)

Introduction: a few brief overview comments, included in most, but not all, sections.

Job Description/Typical Day: the functions, tasks, and responsibilities of a particular job. A specific entry-level job title is provided when possible. This section also describes the life-style implications of the position, including the amount of travel, entertainment, and the working hours that it requires.

Skills and Credentials: the skills, personality traits, interests, work experience, and educational credentials that the position requires.

Compensation: the starting salaries of Harvard and/or University of Virginia MBAs entering this position. The salary information from these schools covers the period from 1979 through 1982, although the most recent year's statistics were used whenever possible. Note that MBAs from Harvard and Darden (UVA) are among the highest paid, so the salaries listed may be above the average paid for that position. Income potential is also provided when available.

Typical Career Path: the future job potential, transferability, and likely advancement route from the entry-level position. A likely time framework for MBAs on a fast track has been provided when available.

Some Employers: a list of possible employers for this type of position. The list includes mostly large, *Fortune* 500 corporations that might recruit at business schools for this position. The location of the corporation's headquarters is shown in parenthesis.

Additional Information: in some reports, covering anything of interest not otherwise provided.

Sources of Additional Information: articles, books, magazines, and the like, where one can learn more about the position and its industry.

The job reports are divided into functional areas and then industries. The Table of Contents provides a helpful cross-reference of related positions and industries.

Unit 1
Functional Positions

6 ASSISTANT TO THE PRESIDENT

Education (degrees)	BA	MBA	PhD
Experience required (yrs)	None	1-3	3+
Location	Urban	Rural	Regional / Travel
Compensation ($/yr)	< $25K	$25-30K	$30-35K / >$35K
Work involvement (hrs/wk)	< 50	50-60	> 60
Pace	Relaxed	Medium	Frenetic
Career path (a la Driver)	Spiral	Steady	Linear
Interpersonal style	Loner	Moderate	Outgoing
Cognitive style	Sequential Rules Details	Mixed Principles Systems	Random Free form Big picture
Variety (preference for)	No change Ordered	Occasional Change	Ambiguous Changing

INTRODUCTION

The position of <u>Assistant to the President (ATP)</u> may vary dramatically in responsibility, life-style, and career potential, depending upon the personalities involved and the circumstances of the corporation. An MBA in this position may have more control over his or her daily routine and contribution to the company than in any other entry-level position. The relationship developed between the President and his or her assistant will affect the range and focus of the ATP's projects, the amount of responsibility involved, the number of hours worked, and the career path that he or she will follow.

Job Description/Typical Day

The scope of activities of an ATP may range from those that are entirely nonbusiness (personal assistance) to those that provide an overview of the business. Business responsibilities may include budget planning, market analysis, troubleshooting divisional problems, supervising newly hired MBAs, strategic planning, providing technical or legal advice, and relieving the boss of office work. Daily activities may include writing reports, attending meetings with the high-level executives, traveling with the President, on-the-job training, and making decisions when the President is away.

The routine and life-style depend upon the boss and the nature of the position, that is, whether it is a training ground for new MBAs or a middle management spot leading to a top executive position. Hours range from 40 to 55 per week and travel ranges from 0 to 25 percent.

Skills

The most important skills needed for this position are interpersonal and communicative ones, followed by a sensitivity to politics, a tolerance for ambiguous, unstructured situations, and the ability to be flexible and to develop and start one's own projects. An ATP must also be creative and willing to take risks.

Compensation

The compensation for ATPs varies depending upon the size of the firm and the importance of the position within the firm. Our review showed salaries ranging from $18,000 to $30,000 in 1981. Small companies may include profit sharing or other top executive perks as a sweetener.

Typical Career Paths

The job duration for the ATP is usually one to two years. After that, promotional opportunities usually lead in one of two directions. The ATP may be offered a position on one of the corporate staffs (i.e., financial, strategic planning) or may be offered a line position with one of the divisions. The line position is often seen as a stepping stone to further advancement within the division. It is important to note, however, that there is no standard career path for the ATP. If you find yourself working in such a position, keep your eyes and ears open for opportunities that fit your skills. You are in a unique position to see the opportunities available within the entire corporation, and your opportunity is often the one you choose.

Very little information has been provided on career opportunities for the ATP in switching firms. Nevertheless, conversations with one ATP have revealed that the attribute for which he was originally hired—raw talent—combined with the prestige of the ATP position made staff positions with other companies an excellent possibility. Consulting firms were also mentioned as a potential new employer. One's attractiveness to consulting firms or other companies, however, would be highly dependent on the scope and level of responsibility held as an ATP.

Some Employers

Likely employers or those who have recruited for this position in the past include the following:

Acton Corporation (Acton, Massachusetts)
American Can (Greenwich, Connecticut)
American Home Products (New York, New York)
Ashland Oil (Ashland, Kentucky)
Bendix Corporation (Southfield, Michigan)
Cummins Engine (Columbus, Indiana)
W. R. Grace (New York, New York)
Mark Twain Bankshares (St. Louis, Missouri)
E. W. Moran Drilling Company (Midland, Texas)
Norton Simon (New York, New York)
Principal Group Limited (Alberta, Canada)
Sunbeam Plastics (Evansville, Indiana)
Vitimins, Inc. (Chicago, Illinois)
White House Fellowships (Washington, D.C.)

Additional Information

The major advantages of this position, as seen by past and present ATPs, are the opportunities to develop a close relationship with top executives; to gain an overview of an entire corporation from "the top"; to be in on, if not actively participate in, strategic decisions; to gain access to important people in and out of the corporation; to specialize in a specific function or to remain a generalist; to create one's own job; and to watch for and help select one's next position in the company.

The major disadvantages of the position are its dependence on the personality of the boss and the relationship that you develop, the resentment that you may face from other senior managers, the difficulty in measuring your results and

performance, the lack of clearly defined authority, and the lack of job security.
For those interested in this position, ATPs recommend the following:

1. Clearly define and discuss your objectives for the job.
2. Be sure of your rapport with the President.
3. Find out the hidden tasks that may be personal and mundane.
4. Determine the extent to which the job is reactive or proactive.
5. Determine whether the ATP position is a permanent, temporary, or new position within the company.
6. Examine your predecessor's next job and how it was determined.

Sources of Additional Information

SHAREWELL, WILLIAM, "Idea Managers—A New Look at Staff vs. Line Jobs," *Management Review,* August 1978, p. 24.
SMITH, PAULA, "The Vanishing Executive Assistant," *Duns Review,* June 1974, p. 86.
URWICK, L. F., "The Assistant-to: Problem Child of Business," *Management Review*, March 1974, p. 27.

7 CORPORATE FINANCIAL MANAGEMENT

	BA	MBA	PhD
Education (degrees)	BA	MBA	PhD
Experience required (yrs)	None	1-3	3+
Location	Urban	Rural	Regional / Travel
Compensation ($/yr)	$< $25K	$25-30K	$30-35K / $>$35K
Work involvement (hrs/wk)	$< 50	50-60	$> 60
Pace	Relaxed	Medium	Frenetic
Career path (a la Driver)	Spiral	Steady	Linear
Interpersonal style	Loner	Moderate	Outgoing
Cognitive style	Sequential Rules Details	Mixed Principles Systems	Random Free form Big picture
Variety (preference for)	No change Ordered	Occasional Change	Ambiguous Changing

Job Description/Typical Day

An MBA typically begins in corporate finance as a <u>Financial Analyst</u>. This is a staff position; that is, the analyst acts primarily as a financial advisor to decision makers higher in the chain of command. Assignments are generally short term, involve incorporation of financial details, and have deadlines for completion. Much of the work involves routine management of the firm's financial resources—cash management, preparation of budgets, and construction of pro forma financial statements. Other activities may involve review of contracts, analysis of acquisition candidates, lease/buy analyses, and financial analysis of competitors. The analyst deals with the capital markets only on occasion, except in large corporations that constantly engage in rate swaps, hedging and arbitrage, and the purchase and sale of securities. Most firms go for long periods without seeking external financing. Thus, the primary focus of the analyst, at least at the start, is within the corporation.

The foregoing description is probably most valid for large firms with formal policy development processes. In small firms, tasks and routines are more varied, less structured, and maybe a bit more outwardly focused.

At the entry level, the corporate Financial Analyst can be located almost anywhere in the country, although he or she tends to be located in metropolitan areas. The position entails fairly regular work hours, with some periods of overtime work expected during busy periods (capital budgeting, new project appropriations, etc.). The analyst generally maintains a stable life-style as he or she progresses, being promoted several times throughout his or her career and sometimes "serving time" at a divisional location. There may be some travel to the divisions, but most of the corporate analyst's work is done at headquarters.

The position to which Financial Analysts aspire is the Chief Financial Officer (CFO). The CFO has usually worked up through the organization from the entry-level position, having changed companies perhaps once in his or her career. Although current CFOs are considerably more mobile than their predecessors were, there is comparatively less mobility required in this functional area than in some others (i.e., marketing). With many corporations assuming an international focus, the CFO may well do a lot of traveling, within the United States and overseas. He or she must have an active interest in keeping up with modern financial techniques. Some large corporations (Exxon, General Motors, Ford) use the Treasurer's office to develop future general managers for the highest positions within the company.

Skills

A Financial Manager should be a self-starter, someone who does not need a lot of direct supervision. Communication skills are crucial, since the staff nature of the finance function requires persuading others in the organization to accept one's conclusions. Financial Managers frequently refer to themselves as "salesmen" in this regard. It is important to be comfortable with details, but not be obsessed with them. Math skills are obviously important, as is feeling comfortable pushing numbers, especially early in one's career.

What is the typical Financial Manager like? *Development of Financial Managers* by Schiller et al., Financial Executives Research Foundation, sheds some light on the question, although the study was done a decade ago. A typical financial manager is a "relatively reserved and cautious individual who shows a strong desire to handle broad leadership responsibilities while still maintaining the tendency to become personally involved in some of the details of his work" (p. 25). The more successful financial managers tend to be delegators, not doers; they are self-confident and have a broad viewpoint.

Compensation

Financial Analyst entry level	$20,000–25,000
Middle management levels	$30,000–40,000
Upper management levels	$40,000–100,000

Usual benefits include stock options, bonuses (upper levels), medical coverage, insurance and, often, savings plans.

Typical Career Paths

The premier financial position in a corporation is that of Vice President, Finance or Chief Financial Officer. The CFO generally reports directly to the President. The CFO has two main functions under his or her auspices: the Treasurer and the Controller. The Treasurer's responsibilities include cash control, bank relations, external financing, and investor relations. The Controller's responsibilities involve internal programs, including tax accounting, financial planning, insurance management, general accounting, auditing, credit management, budgetary control, capital expenditure control, cost accounting, management information systems, and mergers and acquisitions.

A 1975 study found that the average CFO was 50 years old, having spent 15 years with his current firm and 5 years as CFO. Twenty-four percent of all CFOs held MBA degrees. Most CFOs had either treasury or control experience.

The most common advancement routes to the CFO post are (1) promotions via the Controller department; (2) promotions via the Treasurer's department; (3) promotions via the Corporate Planning or the Operations Research departments and then a lateral move to Finance; (4) external entry from an investment bank, commercial bank, consulting firm, or public accounting firm.

Based on current business trends, CFOs and CFO aspirants must emphasize economic forecasting, international monetary control, and interpersonal and generalist skills. He or she has become not only a manager of specialists, but is a stronger contender than ever for the Chief Executive Officer (CEO) post.

Some Employers

All companies need competent financial managers. One measure for determining a company's emphasis on finance is the relative compensation of financial management:

**Top Five Industries by
Salaries of Financial Managers**   **Firms Likely to Be Hiring**

Transportation equipment   All major corporations

Chemicals and petroleum

Paper products

Food products

Transportation

Additional Information

Things to look for in a firm include:

Growth (external financing needs)
Maturity (internal control needs)
Competitive position (greater emphasis on financial demands)
Financial statements (problem-solving profile)
Backgrounds of CEO and CFO
Existence of training programs

Sources of Additional Information

Magazines

Business Week
The Financial Executive
Forbes
Fortune
Harvard Business Review

Newspapers

Barron's
Financial Analyst's Journal
Financial Times (UK)
The Wall Street Journal

Financial Executives Research Foundation. *Development of Financial Managers,* 1970

8 CORPORATE PLANNING

Education (degrees)	BA	MBA	PhD
Experience required (yrs)	None	1-3	3+
Location	Urban	Rural	Regional / Travel
Compensation ($/yr)	< $25K	$25-30K	$30-35K / >$35K
Work involvement (hrs/wk)	< 50	50-60	> 60
Pace	Relaxed	Medium	Frenetic
Career path (a la Driver)	Spiral	Steady	Linear
Interpersonal style	Loner	Moderate	Outgoing
Cognitive style	Sequential Rules Details	Mixed Principles Systems	Random Free form Big picture
Variety (preference for)	No change Ordered	Occasional Change	Ambiguous Changing

Job Description/Typical Day

Corporate planning is a broad job classification that may mean different things depending on the size, structure, and goals of the particular organization. Most positions contain elements of one or more of the functional activities listed in the paragraphs that follow, although content of the individual position may vary greatly.

Corporate development involves the analysis of possible mergers, acquisitions, divestitures, or candidates for development.

Corporate economics involves monitoring and interpreting the corporation's external economic environment, including the national economy, industries served, and the competition. This area prepares annual economic forecasts for use in preparing divisional strategic plans.

Planning systems involves designing, implementing, and maintaining a strategic planning system. The importance of planning must be sold to top management by this group.

Business planning involves reviewing and critiquing strategic plans throughout the annual planning cycle and evaluating the performance of the operating divisions.

Corporate Planners work in a relatively unstructured environment, so there is some freedom in selecting the projects undertaken and the process for completing them. The work load is moderate (40 to 50 hours per week) except for occasional rush projects. Travel is limited, and the planner spends approximately 60 percent of his or her time alone analyzing data.

The corporate planning job has high visibility and, therefore, allows frequent exposure to senior and line management. Turnover, which is high, can give planners constant exposure to new ideas but also frustration as they leave the department before seeing the results of their work.

Skills

Corporate Planners must be able to process large amounts of data, extract the key points, and integrate them into a useful form. They must have strong communicative skills and be sensitive to the goals and culture of the organization. Extensive knowledge of at least one of the following areas is necessary: financial analysis, economics, forecasting, business modeling, management science, and computer systems.

Compensation

Entry-level salaries for MBAs are competitive with other entry-level corporate jobs in finance or marketing ($30,000 plus).

Typical Career Paths

Corporate planning is seldom a career, for a full-time planner would have little credibility. Either at the entry level or later in one's career a typical tenure in the planning area is two or three years. From planning, the next job is a line position in the corporation. A stint in planning in later years is usually at the discretion of management, to provide additional experience in preparation for further line responsibility. Whether at the entry level or as an interim position between line assignments, a planning position provides good experience and high visibility.

Some Employers

Formal planning departments exist in large corporations such as Exxon, Xerox, General Electric, and American Express. However, the broadest responsibility and best opportunity may lie with an emerging company where one could develop a special position.

Additional Information

The planning function can offer an attractive mix of visibility, overview of the company's business, opportunity to utilize technical MBA skills, room for achievement, and reasonable work load. Each position must be researched carefully, however, to avoid a possible "Bermuda Triangle." Consider the corporate culture. Is management committed to the planning process? What do other people in the corporation think of the planning department's work? Are the company's actions consistent with expressed strategy? What happens to Corporate Planners when they leave the department? If the Corporate Planning department is indeed an integral part of the company, your chances for advancement will be greatly enhanced.

Sources of Additional Information

"Corporate Strategists Under Fire," *Fortune*, December 27, 1982, p. 34.
OHMAE, KENICHI. "The 'Strategic Triangle' and Business Unit Strategy," *The McKinsey Quarterly,* Winter 1983, p. 9.

9 PERSONNEL/HUMAN RESOURCES

	BA	MBA	PhD
Education (degrees)	BA	MBA	PhD
Experience required (yrs)	None	1-3	3+
Location	Urban	Rural	Regional / Travel
Compensation ($/yr)	< $25K	$25-30K	$30-35K / >$35K
Work involvement (hrs/wk)	< 50	50-60	> 60
Pace	Relaxed	Medium	Frenetic
Career path (a la Driver)	Spiral	Steady	Linear
Interpersonal style	Loner	Moderate	Outgoing
Cognitive style	Sequential Rules Details	Mixed Principles Systems	Random Free form Big picture
Variety (preference for)	No change Ordered	Occasional Change	Ambiguous Changing

INTRODUCTION

The personnel function is generally considered to be growing in importance with the acceleration of such trends as increased government mandates and increased concern for human resources management and the quality of work life. According to a report by the Bureau of Labor Statistics, the personnel function is near the top of growing occupations. Demand for people in the personnel function is expected to increase 40 percent in the next decade, a coming phase that is being characterized by some as "the people era" in management concentration.

Job Description/Typical Day

The role of a Personnel Manager, or Human Resources Manager, is to provide assistance to other members of the management team regarding the best use of the people belonging to that organization. Well over half of the personnel managers in the United States are employed by private businesses and industries, but many also are employed by government agencies, educational institutions, and public utilities. The specific duties of a Human Resources Manager depend on the nature and size of the organization in which he or she is employed. In large corporate settings, managers are responsible for several specialized areas: employment (recruiting and placement), training and career development, compensation and benefits administration, employee and labor relations, and safety.

Human Resources Managers typically work in comfortable, pleasant surroundings. Their hours are fairly regular, with occasional overtime due to circumstances such as employment buildups or work stoppages. Employee and labor relations specialists, however, may work many overtime hours because of labor strikes and negotiations.

Skills

Human Resources Managers are specialists and generalists. As specialists, they need technical skills, particularly in compensation and benefits administration, training, and employee and labor relations. (Labor relations specialists often have law degrees.) As generalists, they need strong interpersonal and communication skills. Additionally, they should be able to propose policies that maximize the organization's profit and that protect the worker's welfare.

Compensation

The typical Personnel Manager earns a little less than $30,000 annually, while upper-level corporate professionals may earn from $40,000 to $100,000 annually depending on their responsibilities. In two *Wall Street Journal* surveys, (February 15, 1983, p. 1 and April 26, 1983, p. 1), Personnel Managers have led the way in percentage salary increases for the past two years. Benefits in larger corporations usually include life and health insurance, retirement plans, profit-sharing plans, paid vacations, and educational assistance.

Typical Career Paths

Within the HRM Function. In most companies, the Human Resources Manager will need to develop a wide range of skills to enable lateral movement within the function. Career advancement may also be possible if the HRM chooses to build up and expand the HR department itself.

Outside the HRM Function. Historically, unless one possessed skills in another functional area, it has been difficult to make lateral moves within a corporation. This is changing, as we see with Exxon's and Hewlett-Packard's willingness to shift employees to new departments within a single firm.

Another telling trend is the number of CEOs with a background in personnel, such as those of Cummins Engine, Delta, Royal Dutch Shell, and International Paper.

Some Employers

Firms with innovative personnel programs include:

American Hospital Supply (Evanston, Illinois)
Bendix (Southfield, Michigan)
Cummins Engine (Columbus, Indiana)
Delta (Atlanta, Georgia)
Digital Equipment Corp. (Maynard, Massachusetts)
Exxon (New York)
Hewlett-Packard (Palo Alto, California)
Kodak (Rochester, New York)
Wells Fargo (San Francisco, California)
Westvaco (New York)
Xerox (New York)

Additional Information

While employers need good Human Resources Managers, they may not recruit them actively, even at leading graduate business schools. Consequently, the applicant bears more of the responsibility for finding a job in the field. Promotional materials, other than annual reports, reflect the attention given to personnel management and indicate the availability of training programs for employees.

Sources of Additional Information

The Directory of Career Training and Development Programs, published by Ready Reference Press in Santa Monica, names organizations that have training and development programs and/or active interest in new personnel workers. See James W. Walker, *Human Resource Planning* (New York: McGraw-Hill, 1980), and Ed Schein, *Career Dynamics* (Reading, Mass.: Addison-Wesley, 1978), for more information on what personnel jobs entail.

10 PRODUCT MANAGEMENT

INTRODUCTION

The Product Manager (PM) is the coordinator of all the skills and tasks necessary to bring a product to market and to sell it. The position is characterized by a high level of responsibility (typically for the profit and loss statement) and a low level of authority. Most of a PM's time is spent motivating, negotiating, and gathering and transferring information. Approximately half of a PM's time is spent in meetings.

The terms used in different companies to describe this function are product management, brand management, and (occasionally) program management, among others. The type of products managed by people in this function range from highly image- and advertising-dependent consumer products, such as cosmetics or alcoholic beverages; to packaged consumer goods, such as foods or household products; to hybrid consumer/technological products (e.g., Texas Instruments' "Speak and Spell"); to purely technological, industrial goods (e.g., computer systems).

Within the product/brand group, people work as a team on the same projects or problems, although day-to-day responsibilities vary according to one's level and the "size" or importance of the brand or product. Entry-level positions emphasize more administrative work; the higher up a person goes, the more he or she is involved in planning. The more junior levels within the product management structure tend to have more contact with other people throughout the organization, serving as the focal points of myriad staff functions (research and development, market research, manufacturing, sales, advertising agency, finance, and legal) without having direct line authority over these functions.

The trends in product management are toward more MBAs; a more "generalist" emphasis; more female product managers; more entrepreneurial managers, who are risk takers; and less centralized decision-making power.

The following sections examine product management positions for consumer, industrial, and high-technology products.

PRODUCT MANAGEMENT: CONSUMER

Education (degrees)	BA	MBA	PhD
Experience required (yrs)	None	1-3	3+
Location	Urban	Rural	Regional / Travel
Compensation ($/yr)	< $25K	$25-30K	$30-35K / >$35K
Work involvement (hrs/wk)	< 50	50-60	> 60
Pace	Relaxed	Medium	Frenetic
Career path (a la Driver)	Spiral	Steady	Linear
Interpersonal style	Loner	Moderate	Outgoing
Cognitive style	Sequential Rules Details	Mixed Principles Systems	Random Free form Big picture
Variety (preference for)	No change Ordered	Occasional Change	Ambiguous Changing

Typical Day/Job Description

The entry-level position for an MBA in consumer product management is as a Marketing Assistant or Assistant Product Manager. The typical tasks performed at this and the next, Associate, level include forecasting of sales and profits, budgeting, developing new product extensions, assisting and planning promotional and advertising campaigns, setting up local test markets, training subordinates, and developing packages.

Work hours average forty-five to fifty per week, and travel varies with the particular job and company. Product Managers are stationed in their company's headquarters, which are usually in large urban areas. Initial field sales training may be required, however, involving three or more months away from the home office. The work environment is highly people and group oriented. The primary sources of dissatisfaction mentioned by Product Managers are long hours, high pressure, and the lack of decision-making authority for several years.

Skills

Product management requires strong interpersonal skills, the ability to work in small groups, and the ability to take on responsibility without line authority. Analytical skills, the ability to plan in the short and long run, quantitative skills, and the ability to organize one's own time effectively are also essential. Product Managers see themselves as creative, confident, responsible, aggressive, perceptive, organized, energetic, independent, and goal oriented.

Compensation

Our review shows salaries ranging from $25,000 to $35,000.

Typical Career Paths

In many companies with a product management structure, marketing is *the* function and is, therefore, the best entry into top management. Competition for promotions is keen. Many companies have an "up-or-out" policy to make room for more recently hired talent. There is significant lateral movement between brands; such a move can serve as a promotion if it is to a "bigger" brand (in terms of advertising and promotional dollars, size of brand group, sales volume, strategic importance to the company, etc.).

There is significant opportunity to move outside the company any time after approximately two years of training. This is especially true of some of the larger companies with good training programs.

Typical Career Path

Marketing Assistant/Assistant Product Manager	12 to 18 months*
Assistant/Associate Product Manager	24 to 30 months

*These time frames vary considerably by size and sophistication of the product management structure.

Product Manager   24 to 70 months
Group Product Manager
Marketing Director
Vice-President
Group Vice-President
Executive Vice-President
President

Alternative career paths are manager of overseas marketing division, domestic marketing staff position, and general management positions in a corporate affiliate or subsidiary.

The skills developed in consumer product management are excellent for general management, and therefore, movement into this area is quite free. It is more difficult, however, to move from consumer to industrial product management.

Some Employers

Bristol-Myers (New York, New York)
Clorox (Oakland, California)
Frito-Lay (Dallas, Texas)
General Foods (White Plains, New York)
General Mills (Minneapolis, Minnesota)
Gillette (Boston, Massachusetts)
Johnson & Johnson (New Brunswick, New Jersey)
Eli Lilly (Indianapolis, Indiana)
Pfizer (New York, New York)
Pillsbury (Minneapolis, Minnesota)
Procter & Gamble (Cincinnati, Ohio)
Quaker Oats (Chicago, Illinois)

Sources of Additional Information

See the following magazines:

Advertising Age
Direct Marketing
Journal of Marketing
Marketing and Media Decisions
Sales & Marketing Monthly

PRODUCT MANAGEMENT: HIGH TECHNOLOGY

	BA	MBA	PhD
Education (degrees)	BA	MBA	PhD
Experience required (yrs)	None	1-3	3+
Location	Urban	Rural	Regional / Travel
Compensation ($/yr)	< $25K	$25-30K	$30-35K / >$35K
Work involvement (hrs/wk)	< 50	50-60	> 60
Pace	Relaxed	Medium	Frenetic
Career path (a la Driver)	Spiral	Steady	Linear
Interpersonal style	Loner	Moderate	Outgoing
Cognitive style	Sequential Rules Details	Mixed Principles Systems	Random Free form Big picture
Variety (preference for)	No change Ordered	Occasional Change	Ambiguous Changing

Job Description/Typical Day

In high-technology companies, the PM generally spends more time with customers than in consumer or industrial marketing, especially if the company's customer base is narrow. This customer contact is necessary because product life cycles are shorter, product obsolescence can be a continual threat, and timing of new product introductions vis-à-vis competitors is critical.

Through customer contacts, the PM identifies unmet customer needs, gains ideas for new product applications, and ensures that customers are properly trained to use the product. In the case of very specialized or expensive products, the PM may be required to obtain customer commitment before a development program or production can begin. During the introductory phase, the PM is often responsible for training and educating the sales force in the uses of the product, which can be complex.

More market planning is required of a PM in high-technology firms because of the greater risk of obsolescence; the PM strives to anticipate market and technological changes.

The PM's tasks typically include financial analysis, pricing, marketing planning, customer contact, working with technical staff on scheduling and product improvements, training and assisting salespeople, packaging, and coordinating all functional areas.

As with consumer and industrial product management, "Hi Tech" PMs have fairly regular hours.

While travel requirements vary, PMs tend to travel two to ten days per month, not only because they are very involved with the customers and sales force during the introduction of new products, but also because they must constantly stay attuned to their customers' needs.

PMs report that this is a very-high-pressure job and that there is fierce competition for assignments to the products with the greatest profit potential. In some companies, a newcomer to Hi Tech feels pressure to "prove" himself or herself.

Sources of dissatisfaction for Hi Tech PMs include lack of authority, pressure, frustration, "firefighting," and factors beyond their control affecting performance evaluations.

Skills

People Skills. These include motivating, negotiating, and persuading. Some PMs describe Hi Tech firms as more performance oriented and internally less political.

Communicating Skills. Essential are knowing how to ask the right questions, knowing how to write and speak effectively, and knowing when to use which skill.

Analytical/Financial Skills.   The PM must be able to evaluate profitability, budget, and make sales forecasts.

Technical Credibility.   This is very important in a Hi Tech firm. While a technical background is not required, it is essential that a PM be able to understand the product thoroughly. The depth of knowledge required depends on whether the company is market or engineering driven and on the expectations of the customers. Technical expertise is necessary when dealing with original equipment manufacturers and engineering-oriented firms. Industry knowledge is more useful when the product is targeted at end users and applications-oriented firms, although technical knowledge may also be necessary in this case.

High-technology firms are beginning to emphasize business and interpersonal skills over technical skills in their recruiting process. There is a trend in Hi Tech firms toward dividing product management tasks according to the skills required during different phases of development:

Job	Task	Skills Required
Product planning Product management Technical/ marketing	Conceives idea Coordinates development and introduction	Technical
Product marketing	Positioning, sales growth, maintenance, marketing	Marketing

Compensation

The salary range is very wide: "typical" salaries might be anywhere from $25,000 to $50,000. Salary varies with degree of responsibility, compatibility of background with the product offering, and experience.

Benefits also vary enormously. When new products are introduced in foreign countries, PMs have the opportunity to travel. In smaller companies, stock options or profit-sharing options might be offered in lieu of salary, particularly if the PM brings a great deal of expertise to the company.

Typical Career Paths

There are two distinguishing characteristics of product management in a high-technology firm: (1) because of the rapid growth of these firms, advancement can be fairly rapid; (2) because product management is considered a training ground for upper (general) management and because a Hi Tech company is not completely market driven, transfers between functions are encouraged. In the career paths that follow, "lateral move" indicates a move to another function: sales, strategic planning or where appropriate, finance or engineering.

Representative Career Path	Alternate Career Path
Assistant Product Manager (1 to 2 years)	Assistant Product Manager Product Manager

Product Manager (1 to 2 years)
Possible lateral move
Group Manager (2 to 4 years)
Lateral move
Upper management

Engineering Product Manager (if background appropriate)
Group Manager (or a Product Manager may stay on the technical track instead of returning to marketing)
Upper management

Some Employers

Large employers include:

Data General Corp. (Westboro, Massachusetts)
Digital Equipment Corp. (Maynard, Massachusetts)
Genrad, Inc. (Concord, Massachusetts)
Hewlett-Packard Co. (Palo Alto, California)
Intel Corp. (Santa Clara, California)
Texas Instruments (Dallas, Texas)

Additional Information

PMs in high-technology companies generally agree that (1) their job requires a great deal of interaction with engineering-oriented people, and (2) it is essential that a PM like the technology with which he or she will be dealing.

Sources of Additional Information

See Product Management: Industrial (pp. 62).

PRODUCT MANAGEMENT: INDUSTRIAL

Education (degrees)	BA	MBA	PhD
Experience required (yrs)	None	1-3	3+
Location	Urban	Rural	Regional / Travel
Compensation ($/yr)	< $25K	$25-30K	$30-35K / >$35K
Work involvement (hrs/wk)	< 50	50-60	> 60
Pace	Relaxed	Medium	Frenetic
Career path (a la Driver)	Spiral	Steady	Linear
Interpersonal style	Loner	Moderate	Outgoing
Cognitive style	Sequential Rules Details	Mixed Principles Systems	Random Free form Big picture
Variety (preference for)	No change Ordered	Occasional Change	Ambiguous Changing

Job Description/Typical Day

In contrast to consumer product management, industrial product management involves less market research, less advertising, and more customer contact. The main activities include pricing, promotional, packaging, product line decisions, sales forecasting, determining channels of distribution, preparation for trade shows, and strategic planning input.

The work environment is unstructured, supervision is minimal, and job descriptions are often vague. Product Managers interface with all functional areas and have access to high-level management, which brings high visibility.

Hours are regular and involve some entertainment and travel to customers and trade shows.

Skills

Industrial Product Managers require good interpersonal skills, persuasive ability, organizational skill, and the ability to work with little supervision. Some companies may require technical skill or sales experience. An entrepreneurial and generalist inclination is helpful as is adaptability to a constantly changing environment.

Compensation

Compensation is "competitive," with salaries for entry-level positions ranging from $23,000 to $31,000. Foreign opportunities go as high as $45,000; however, most companies require experience for salaries in the higher ranges.

According to a 1980 study in the *Executive Compensation: Fourteenth Survey* (Chicago: Dartnell Corporation, 1982), Product Managers were paid an average total compensation of $24,000 for companies in the under-$5 million sales range contrasted to $49,000 for corporations with $500 million to $1 billion in annual sales volume. Twenty to sixty-six percent of the Product Managers gained incentive compensation. Note that this report does not distinguish Industrial from Consumer Product Managers.

Typical Career Paths

The following are four possible career paths. The nature of the path within a company results from the company's size, the size of the particular product's sales versus total sales, the industry, and the focus of the company (marketing, sales, or production). In some companies, a Product Manager will move laterally from product to product prior to moving up the ladder.

1. Assistant Product Manager (6 to 12 months)
   Product Specialist (staff, 6 to 12 months)
   Product Manager
   Marketing Manager
   General Management

2. Product Manager-Product Line Manager-Division Manager
3. Sales (2 years)-Product Manager-Head of Marketing in a division
4. Product Assistant
   Assistant Product Manager
   Product Manager
   Product Line Manager
   Vice-President, Small Business Unit

Some Employers

Representative employers include:

Chemicals

Air Products & Chemical (Allentown, Pennsylvania)
Ciba-Geigy Ltd. (Ardsley, New York)
Du Pont (Wilmington, Delaware)

Communications

AT&T Long Lines (New York, New York)
Western Electric (New York, New York)

Computers

Data General Corp. (Westboro, Massachusetts)
Datapoint Corp. (San Antonio, Texas)
Digital Equipment Corp. (Maynard, Massachusetts)
Intel Corp. (Santa Clara, California)
Prime Computer (Natick, Massachusetts)

Electrical/Electronic

International Harvester (Chicago, Illinois)
Millipore Corp. (Bedford, Massachusetts)
Rogers Corp. (Rogers, Connecticut)
Textronix Inc. (Beaverton, Oregon)
Varian Associates (Palo Alto, California)

Machinery/Equipment/Systems

Avery International (San Marino, California)
Graco, Inc. (Minneapolis, Minnesota)
Harris Corp. (Melbourne, Florida)
Illinois Tool Works (Chicago, Illinois)
International Harvester (Chicago, Illinois)

Medical

American Hospital Supply (Evanston, Illinois)
Baxter Travenal Labs (Deerfield, Illinois)
Corning Glass Works (Corning, New York)

Transportation

Eaton Corp. (Cleveland, Ohio)
Ford Motor Co. (Detroit, Michigan)
General Motors (Detroit, Michigan)
B. F. Goodrich (Akron, Ohio)
TRW (Cleveland, Ohio)
Millipore Corp. (Bedford, Massachusetts)

Additional Information

Sixty-eight percent of Industrial Product Managers have less than five years
of experience with their current product. Seventy-one percent have been a Product
Manager for less than five years.

Sources of Additional Information

BRITT, STEUART, ed.   *Dartnell Marketing Managers Handbook,* Chicago, Dartnell Corpo-
ration, 1973.
BUELL, VICTOR, ed.   *Handbook of Modern Marketing*, New York, McGraw-Hill, 1970.
Industrial Marketing Management

11 PRODUCTION AND OPERATIONS MANAGEMENT

INTRODUCTION

Because world trade is increasingly important to the American economy, manufacturing is more than ever a competitive weapon in world markets. Companies are looking for ways in which to upgrade their manufacturing management and increase their competitive edge. Use of electronic technologies by foreign competitors is pressuring manufacturers to upgrade their equipment or be left behind. An MBA in the production job has high visibility (would you pay somebody twice what a job was worth and then not watch them?) and is well positioned for movement to top management jobs.

There are two paths to follow in production management, through line and staff positions. Line experience is essential to the MBA aspiring to a general management position, yet staff positions draw more heavily on MBA skills. These paths often cross, and many MBAs will gain experience in both areas during their careers. Engineering or other technical or production experience is a great advantage but is not required. Those without a technical background are more likely to enter staff positions. Those without production experience can look at larger firms, some of which have year-long training programs moving people through all areas of production management before assigning a specific position of responsibility; these positions can be negotiated.

PRODUCTION: LINE

	BA	MBA	PhD
Education (degrees)	BA	MBA	PhD
Experience required (yrs)	None	1-3	3+
Location	Urban	Rural	Regional / Travel
Compensation ($/yr)	< $25K	$25-30K	$30-35K / >$35K
Work involvement (hrs/wk)	< 50	50-60	> 60
Pace	Relaxed	Medium	Frenetic
Career path (a la Driver)	Spiral	Steady	Linear
Interpersonal style	Loner	Moderate	Outgoing
Cognitive style	Sequential Rules Details	Mixed Principles Systems	Random Free form Big picture
Variety (preference for)	No change Ordered	Occasional Change	Ambiguous Changing

Job Description/Typical Day

Advancement to general management usually requires some training experience in production as a First-Line Supervisor (FLS). The FLS supervises a group of workers in a factory environment. He or she schedules workers and machines, handles personnel and union problems, and improvises as necessary to meet production deadlines. The FLS works under short time frame pressures and is not involved in corporate planning and decision making.

Because the FLS implements, rather than dictates, policy, methods, and other production decisions, his or her routine requires little imagination. Those who do use imagination and initiative in handling the day-to-day problems (machine/line breakdowns, process problems, scheduling issues) stand out in a crowd. Let's face it; this MBA is not being hired as an FLS to maintain the status quo. This can be accomplished with a cheaper BA in history. The FLS is often squeezed by pressures from unions on one side and dictated corporate goals on the other. The job mainly consists, therefore, of crisis control, and the FLS can expect far more responsibility than actual authority or control.

This position has definite life-style implications that differ from those of most MBA entry-level positions. The FLS is often required to work odd shifts, odd days, and strict hours and can be "on call" continuously. His or her peers are most often considerably older, almost always male, and mostly from a blue-collar background; they are experienced workers who have been promoted to that job, often as a terminal position. Some industries and companies use the FLS as an entry position for college graduates. The MBA is uncommon. The job usually provides no travel and locations include such places as Moline, Illinois. The highly structured environment and the short-term orientation, however, allow the FLS to leave his or her work at the plant when the workday is over.

Skills

The key required skills are an ability to supervise people with nonprofessional backgrounds, resistance to stress, ability to operate under short time frame pressures and crises, flexibility and adaptability to quickly moving situations, decision-making ability, and sound judgment under duress.

Compensation

The normal pay range for this job might be from $15,000 to $25,000. An MBA hired into this job, however, can expect to be overpaid for the job, to approximately $30,000 to $35,000. (And $30,000 goes a long way in Moline, Illinois.)

Typical Career Paths

Career opportunities are the real reason for an MBA to seek a production supervisor job or for a company to hire an MBA into one. Many, if not most, manufacturing companies consider the FLS job to be the key developmental

experience in a career in line operating management. Many heavily manu-
facturing-oriented companies will keep MBAs out of the manufacturing area
altogether unless the MBA can get experience (even if it's only for six months) as
an FLS. It is because the experience is considered developmental that companies
so often are willing to overpay MBAs in relation to the normal pay range for the
job.

The normal progression in line management is from Foreman (6 to 18
months), to Department Supervisor/Shift Supervisor/General Foreman to Superin-
tendent, to Plant Manager, to Division General Manager or Regional Operations
Manager. Responsibilities, up to the Plant Manager level, are as follows:

Foreman	**Department Manager**
Safety effectiveness	Labor Relations effectiveness
Quality control	Equipment utilization
Housekeeping effectiveness	Production output
Preventive maintenance	Safety effectiveness
Labor relations	Personnel development
Cost control	
Production output (prime)	

Superintendent	**Plant Manager**
Cost control	Personnel planning effectiveness
Labor relations effectiveness	Long-range planning
Interdepartment coordination	General policy development
New start-up effectiveness	Long-range policy determination
New product feasibility	Ingredient control
Personnel development	Material control

MBAs with proven experience in manufacturing, and who show flexibility
and conceptual planning ability, often find themselves welcomed in finance, corporate planning, consulting, and venture capital after their two to five years of
manufacturing experience. Transferability and advancement within a company are
particularly high for those MBAs who clearly explain their desire to use the
production job as a developmental assignment before accepting the company's
offer. Since many firms espouse a "promote from within" policy, however, mobility between firms is restricted compared with other fields.

Sources of Additional Information

See *Supervisory Management* which is a monthly publication of AMACOM.

PRODUCTION: STAFF

	BA	MBA	PhD
Education (degrees)	BA	MBA	PhD
Experience required (yrs)	None	1-3	3+
Location	Urban	Rural	Regional / Travel
Compensation ($/yr)	$< $25K$	$25-30K	$30-35K / $>$35K
Work involvement (hrs/wk)	< 50	50-60	> 60
Pace	Relaxed	Medium	Frenetic
Career path (a la Driver)	Spiral	Steady	Linear
Interpersonal style	Loner	Moderate	Outgoing
Cognitive style	Sequential Rules Details	Mixed Principles Systems	Random Free form Big picture
Variety (preference for)	No change Ordered	Occasional Change	Ambiguous Changing

Job Description/Typical Day

As an alternative to starting in first-line supervision, many MBAs start in staff positions in such areas as manufacturing planning, quality control, and production scheduling. Their duties include inventory control; raw material evaluations; production planning; feasibility studies of make/buy decisions, capital expansion, and staffing; forecasting; improved-process implementation; cost and quality control; and labor relations. Most staff MBA positions are now being geared to develop and deliver systems to assist the manufacturing process. Staff positions in production management tend to involve longer-term problems whereas line positions involve short-term, day-to-day, hour-to-hour problems. There is an emphasis on timely, accurate, and well-thought-out recommendations and implementations.

MBAs in staff positions work more with engineers and other staff members and less with blue-collar workers. Hours are normally regular with little travel required.

Skills

Staff positions require many of the skills learned in business school such as analytical problem-solving skills, decisiveness, detail orientation, and communication skills.

Compensation

Salaries range from $15,000 to $35,000.

Typical Career Paths

A typical career path for an MBA beginning in a production staff position is Production Planning/Quality Control, to Traffic Manager/Buy Materials Manager, to Plant Manager, to Manufacturing executive/Purchasing executive, to Vice-President, Operations.

Employers

Manufacturing includes such a wide and diversified group of businesses that it would take many pages just to list those *likely* to hire. To narrow the search, you might decide on specific industries or segments such as "raw material processor," "fabricator," or "assembler." There are many other ways you can group your choices. Once you have chosen a general grouping, you can help to narrow the search with *Moody's Industrial Manual* and the *Thomas Register.*

Additional Information

Many recruiters sent to business schools are only prepared to discuss staff positions. Therefore, the MBA interested in a line position should write to the company in advance and specify that interest.

Sources of Additional Information

Periodicals

Factory
Industrial Engineering
Industrial Management
Industry Week
Plant Engineering
Production
Production and Inventory Journal

Books

BECKER, CHARLES H. *Plant Managers Handbook,* Englewood Cliffs, New Jersey, Prentice-Hall, 1974.
MAYNARD, HAROLD, ed. *Handbook of Modern Manufacturing Management.* New York, McGraw Hill, 1970.

PRODUCTION MANAGEMENT: HIGH-TECHNOLOGY FIRMS

Education (degrees)	BA	MBA	PhD
Experience required (yrs)	None	1-3	3+
Location	Urban	Rural	Regional / Travel
Compensation ($/yr)	< $25K	$25-30K	$30-35K / >$35K
Work involvement (hrs/wk)	< 50	50-60	> 60
Pace	Relaxed	Medium	Frenetic
Career path (a la Driver)	Spiral	Steady	Linear
Interpersonal style	Loner	Moderate	Outgoing
Cognitive style	Sequential Rules Details	Mixed Principles Systems	Random Free form Big picture
Variety (preference for)	No change Ordered	Occasional Change	Ambiguous Changing

Job Description/Typical Day

MBAs in Hi Tech production usually are involved in production engineering, production management, materials management, or production planning (and scheduling). Movement between these functions is encouraged. There is a short-term perspective in management, at least at the first few levels, with emphasis on keeping the costs of a product down and on smoothly initiating manufacture of new products. These firms typically are growing at over 20 percent per year and have very lean management; every manager must be productive and "staff" are scarce. There is much contact with others, both within Production and with Marketing and Product Engineering. Production managers are involved in many "nuts and bolts" production problems, and an understanding of the product technology helps.

The structure of these companies is "freewheeling" due to high growth rates and short product life cycles. Flexibility is a must. There is value in seeing how all the pieces fit together, but you must be willing to slog through details.

Constant demands placed on one's time by peers and subordinates often make it difficult to complete one's own work. The work typically can be done in a 40-hour week, but involvement and ambition usually force the MBA to devote more like 50 hours to the job. Around "budget time" or during tight production periods, there are work load peaks. High-technology manufacturing does not usually involve the noisy, dirty, stereotypical production environment.

Skills

Technical background and experience are very important, preferably in electrical engineering, though the nontechnical person can usually succeed in the production planning or materials management positions. Because it is necessary to have served in a number of functional areas to be a strong general management candidate, the MBA engineers have the edge. People skills are essential, given the highly unstructured growth environment and the fact that after a couple of promotions an MBA can be managing fifty or one hundred people.

Compensation

For the Harvard class of 1980, the salary range for production jobs was $22,000 to $40,000, with a mean of $29,447. Because of the growth environment and technical requirements, high-technology salaries average a few thousand more than this. According to our sources, a high-technology operations manager five years out of business school is barely making what the management consulting firms offer as starting salaries.

Typical Career Paths

Within the production function, the MBA can typically experience the following progression: Production Engineer, Scheduler, or Production Planner (one year); group-level (ten or so people) Manager (two years); Section-Level (as many as one hundred people) Manager (two years); Plant Functional Manager.

To get to the general management level, it is necessary to make lateral moves to other functions such as marketing and research and development, typically at the section level. It is very difficult for such transfers to take place at the functional management level, so the general management aspirant should not move into a functional management position until he or she is satisfied with the breadth of his or her experience in the company.

We emphasize that high-technology firms encourage cross-functional movement for promising managers. Opportunities are ever present because of the rate of growth. Raises are frequent in the beginning and results are clearly rewarded.

Some Employers

The following high-technology firms have recruited MBAs for production positions in the last three years:

Ampex (Redwood City, California)
Atex Oil Company (Rosewell, New Mexico)
Bendix Corporation (Southfield, Michigan)
Digital Equipment Corp. (Maynard, Massachusetts)
Emerson Electric Company (St. Louis, Missouri)
General Dynamics Corp. (St. Louis, Missouri)
General Electric Company (Fairfield, Connecticut)
Graco Inc. (Minneapolis, Minnesota)
Hewlett-Packard Company (Palo Alto, California)
Intel Corporation (Santa Clara, California)
Mostek Corp. (Carrollton, Texas)
Reliance Electric Co. (Cleveland, Ohio)
Susumu Industrial Co. Ltd. (Kyoto, Japan)
Tektronix, Inc. (Beaverton, Oregon)
Teradyne (Boston, Massachusetts)
Texas Instruments (Dallas, Texas)
Varian Associates (Palo Alto, California)
Xerox Corp. (New York, New York)

International employers include:

Company	Job Location
Abbot Laboratories (North Chicago, Illinois)	Europe, Asia, South America
Ciba-Geigy, Ltd. (Ardsley, New York)	Switzerland
Exxon (New York)	Brazil
Hewlett-Packard (Palo Alto, California)	Europe

Intel Corp. (Santa Clara, California)	Japan
Interactive Data Corp. (Waltham, Massachusetts)	Germany
Janssen Pharmaceutica (Antwerp, Belgium)	Belgium
Millipore Corp. (Bedford, Massachusetts)	Europe
Mostek Corp. (Carrollton, Texas)	Ireland
Olivetti Corp. of America (Tarrytown, New York)	Europe, Asia, South America
Pfizer Inc. (New York)	Europe, Asia, South America
Raychem Corp. (Menlo Park, California)	Europe
Susumu Industrial Co. Ltd. (Kyoto, Japan)	Japan

Additional Information

Of the 1979 Harvard MBAs who went into production, 42 percent had technical backgrounds; the percentage is certainly higher for Hi Tech firms that were responsible for 29 percent of the production jobs taken.

The proportion of women in high-technology production jobs is low, although better than in production jobs as a whole. Our sources cited two factors. First, few women have electrical engineering backgrounds, though their representation is on the rise. Second, high-technology production workers are most usually older women with whom female managers assertedly sometimes have difficulty.

Sources of Additional Information

See Production Management (pp. 66).

12 PROJECT MANAGEMENT

Education (degrees)	BA	MBA	PhD
Experience required (yrs)	None	1-3	3+
Location	Urban	Rural	Regional / Travel
Compensation ($/yr)	< $25K	$25-30K	$30-35K / >$35K
Work involvement (hrs/wk)	< 50	50-60	> 60
Pace	Relaxed	Medium	Frenetic
Career path (a la Driver)	Spiral	Steady	Linear
Interpersonal style	Loner	Moderate	Outgoing
Cognitive style	Sequential Rules Details	Mixed Principles Systems	Random Free form Big picture
Variety (preference for)	No change Ordered	Occasional Change	Ambiguous Changing

INTRODUCTION

Project manager is a generic job title broadly covering two separate areas:

1. Management consulting (see Sections 32–38 on consulting)
2. Management of development projects

Management Consulting derives its generic qualification by virtue of the case approach generally adopted by the larger consulting firm. Management of Development Projects covers the more obvious area of commercial property development, petrochemical and industrial projects, and supervisory and organizational functions.

The data available to us indicate that approximately 70 percent of the jobs offered under the category of project management are for Management Consultants. The remaining 30 percent is divided among companies involved in venture capital, real estate, construction, and more remote consulting services.

Job Description/Typical Day

Since management consulting is covered in detail in another section, we will direct our remarks to the management of development projects.

The activities of a Project Manager include analysis of project viability, preparation of budgets, cost variable analysis, management of commercial property development, review of architectural and engineering specifications, daily project decision making, leasing and tenant relations, and project marketing aspects.

Projects are often several months in duration; thus, changes in work pressures come in spurts, creating a roller coaster effect on one's personal life. Depending upon the assignment, travel can often take you away from home for several nights on end.

Skills

A degree in engineering and experience in construction management can be a big plus, but may not be required. Organizational skills coupled with a solid understanding of managerial finance are important. In the long term, the ability to communicate well and to establish good relationships with a wide variety of people are vital.

Compensation

From discussions with people in the field, we regard a market range for development project positions of $25,000 to $40,000 as realistic.

Benefits vary by company, but they frequently include the usual ones—life insurance, disability, health and hospitalization plan, pension plan, bonus plan, and three weeks' annual vacation.

Typical Career Paths

Career paths are company specific; however, mobility toward other areas of the business are possible with the experience gained in project management. The degree of flexibility and transferability from this position will depend on its status within the corporation.

Some Employers (Development-Oriented Specialists)

Brown & Root Inc. (Houston, Texas)
Manganaro Brothers (Malden, Massachusetts)
Paine Webber Jackson & Curtis (New York, New York)
B. F. Saul & Co. (Chevy Chase, Maryland)
Spaulding & Slye (Burlington, Massachusetts)
Urban Investment and Development Co. (Chicago, Illinois)
Venture Development Group (Houston, Texas)

Sources of Additional Information

Journal of Systems Management
Real Estate Reference Manual
Project Management Quarterly

13   PUBLIC AFFAIRS OFFICE

Education (degrees)	BA	MBA	PhD
Experience required (yrs)	None	1-3	3+
Location	Urban	Rural	Regional / Travel
Compensation ($/yr)	$< $25K	$25-30K	$30-35K / $>$35K
Work involvement (hrs/wk)	$< 50	50-60	$> 60
Pace	Relaxed	Medium	Frenetic
Career path (a la Driver)	Spiral	Steady	Linear
Interpersonal style	Loner	Moderate	Outgoing
Cognitive style	Sequential Rules Details	Mixed Principles Systems	Random Free form Big picture
Variety (preference for)	No change Ordered	Occasional Change	Ambiguous Changing

Job Description/Typical Day

The Public Affairs Office has responsibility for the management of the corporation's relationship with federal, state, and local government, including both legislative and regulatory bodies at each level. Responsibilities, therefore, include gathering information on proposed legislative and regulatory action and communicating it to appropriate corporate officers, coordinating interaction between government and corporate officials, analyzing the economic and other effects of government action, establishing priorities for issue analysis and management, assisting in establishing the corporation's response to issues, and lobbying.

The job requires constant interaction with governmental officials and with other managers in the corporation. You sell your company's position to government officials and your department's work to others in your company. There is a tremendous amount of reading involved, especially close reading of proposed bills and regulations, to which you often will draft your company's response. Most of your time will involve daily contact with information sources, contact with corporate and government officials, and at least preliminary analysis of the impact of government activities on the corporation.

Skills

You must have a fairly sophisticated understanding of the political process. Experience with economic analysis is helpful in assessing the economic impact of proposed government action. Interpersonal skills are needed for the sales capacity of the job.

Compensation

In the corporations reviewed, the heads of public affairs departments ranged from lower-level Vice-Presidents to among the top people in the corporation. Staffs ranged from 1 to 130. Salary, therefore, will vary greatly according to the position in the department and the level of the department in the corporate hierarchy. Dartnell's *Executive Compensation* (1980) reports total compensation means (depending on size of company) for the top Governmental Relations Officer of $40,000 to $72,000, with median ranges from $32,000 to $91,000 (extremely close to what the top Long-Range Planning Executive makes). The median range for a Public Relations Executive (comparable middle staff position) is $31,000 to $43,000.

Typical Career Paths

The future potential of this position for MBAs is its most exciting aspect. Presently, there are few MBAs in the field, and desirable entry-level positions for them are rare. This situation should change, however, as corporations perceive a greater need for a more systematic analysis of governmental influences and the need to incorporate these influences in long-range planning. Most people we talked to expect to see MBAs entering the field in fair numbers in three to five years. Presently, approximately half the public affairs heads we talked to had substantial government experience and were brought in from the outside, and half were from within the company (either line or staff). Many larger companies have begun to rotate fast-track MBAs through the public affairs office for a year or so because senior management considers governmental issues critical. This may bring entry to the field for many MBAs in the near term.

The skills of Public Affairs Officers are transferable to long-range planning and to general management. Few people have advanced to top management from this position, but most people we have talked to expect this to change when more professional management takes over the public affairs function.

Some Employers

Good prospects are companies with regulatory problems, including companies in the following industries: utilities, energy (principally oil and coal), chemicals, drugs, forest products, insurance, banking, and data processing.

Sources of Additional Information

The *Standard & Poor's Directory* will tell you if the company has a Senior Public Affairs Officer. Also, the published membership list of the Public Affairs Council (Washington, D.C.) is a good source of companies with public affairs functions.

14 SALES

	BA	MBA	PhD
Education (degrees)	BA	MBA	PhD
Experience required (yrs)	None	1-3	3+
Location	Urban	Rural	Regional / Travel
Compensation ($/yr)	< $25K	$25-30K	$30-35K / >$35K
Work involvement (hrs/wk)	< 50	50-60	> 60
Pace	Relaxed	Medium	Frenetic
Career path (a la Driver)	Spiral	Steady	Linear
Interpersonal style	Loner	Moderate	Outgoing
Cognitive style	Sequential Rules Details	Mixed Principles Systems	Random Free form Big picture
Variety (preference for)	No change Ordered	Occasional Change	Ambiguous Changing

INTRODUCTION

In the past, a new salesperson was handed a territory and told to sell as much as possible as fast as possible. Now, however, the job requirements have become increasingly complex, and the salesperson is expected to gather market information concerning customer needs and reactions, competition, and appropriate financial packages. In addition, the salesperson is often required to mediate disputes between customers and the credit department and to keep abreast of government regulations. There is a great deal of concern for upgrading salespersons' abilities, especially in finance, and there is now increasing exposure to management. Salespeople have to be more sensitive to profitability than ever before, and there is a growing tendency to evaluate salespeople as individual profit centers.

Selling jobs vary in the number and nature of clients, the amount of travel, and the extent of "cold calling." In general, however, selling involves encounters with different people, tangible results, a lack of structure, high independence, opportunity to move and learn, deal making, some "entrepreneurship," and some technical teaching. On the downside, there is loneliness, pressure, rejection, and paperwork. The job requires energy, commitment, assertiveness, and professionalism. A technical background is not always required, as most companies provide training programs of perhaps three to six months.

Job Description/Typical Day

The selling task varies substantially between industrial and consumer packaged products. Increased computer usage, by both buyer and seller, for identifying industrial supply needs, has made the selling effort for these products less personal and more difficult. Purchasing agents have become far more sophisticated and, likewise, demand technical sophistication from salespeople. The new industrial salesperson must be extremely well informed and professional, as customers rely heavily on his or her technical knowledge and competence.

The high degree of advertising of consumer packaged goods, however, often makes these products presold. The consumer packaged goods salesperson is, therefore, more involved in developing, maintaining, and stocking distribution channels, in conveying promotional information to his or her distributors, introducing new products, and taking customers' orders.

Although sales can make a highly rewarding and lucrative career, most MBAs enter sales for the further entree it provides to sales and/or marketing management. MBAs with prior sales experience may begin directly in sales management.

In most cases, the Sales Manager is not involved in direct selling efforts, except perhaps for key accounts. The manager's main function is to manage the sales team, that is, the product managers, territorial servicing personnel, technical staff, merchandisers, telephone sales staff, and sales administration. Most sales management positions do require time spent in the field visiting lower-level managers and key customers, so there is usually a good deal of travel.

The Sales Manager's overriding concern is the development of the sales team, particularly the people in the field. The task of developing loyalty and motivation demands increasing attention to remuneration policies, incentives, security, status, and job satisfaction. More than anything, the Sales Manager's job is to be a "communicator," both *downward* to the sales force regarding product and price information, company policies, and corporate image and *upward* to management concerning customer reactions, competition, and sales force needs.

As the Sales Manager advances through the organization, his or her responsibilities broaden to include more strategic planning and less management of salespeople. Particularly in the rapidly changing environment of technical and industrial sales, there is a great deal more emphasis on forecasting, information gathering, precise analysis, and profitability planning. The task of developing training programs in finance and profitability analysis for salespeople has likewise become more important.

Skills

The primary skill required for sales is an ability to deal effectively with people. The friendly, easygoing manner of a good salesperson is more a personality trait than a learned skill. Other skills that are needed include persuasiveness, persistence, assertiveness, empathy, and a goal orientation. In addition to these, a Sales Manager must have the ability to organize, plan, and motivate.

Compensation

Sales compensation can be categorized as lower than average in the early stages with higher than average potential. Consumer packaged goods salespeople's salaries begin at around $18,000 to $20,000, although this will vary with the level of experience. Industrial sales may pay slightly more depending upon the salesperson's technical background and sales experience.

A portion of compensation is usually tied to sales results, either through a commission or bonus. The more complicated and technologically sophisticated the product, the less compensation will be tied to sales results. Commissions or sales bonuses will continue for those progressing into the midlevel sales management positions.

Perks include company cars, free meals, expense accounts, and travel to sales conventions.

The following are approximate salary ranges for one large consumer packaged product firm.

	Salary	**Bonus**
Sales Representative	$17,000–19,000	Up to 25% of total income
Area Manager	$30,000	"

District Manager $40,000–65,000   ″
Regional Sales Manager   ″
Division Vice-President $60,000–$100,000   ″

Typical Career Paths

For many technical product salespeople or manufacturers' representatives, the sales position is the beginning and end of their careers. Their progression might be in terms of improved territories, larger and more sophisticated clients, or better and more lucrative products. Successful salespeople can enjoy a rewarding career and a comfortable life-style on a six-figure income.

For those using sales as an entree to management, representative career paths might be as follows:

Consumer Product Sales

Position	Duties	Tenure
Sales Representative	Supervise 1 salesrep	1½ to 2 years
Service Representative	Supervise 6 to 8 sales managers	1½ to 2 years
Area Sales Representative	Supervise 40 to 50 salesreps	1½ years plus*
District/Territory Manager	Supervise 3 to 5 regions	
Regional Sales Manager		
Division Vice-President		

Industrial Sales

Sales Representative
District Manager
Regional Manager
Zone Manager
National Sales Manager
Vice-President of Marketing or Sales
Chief Operating Officer of Marketing or Sales

Upward mobility into top executive positions is heavily dependent upon the importance that the company places on sales. Marketing often carries more status and is the grooming area for top management. Transfer into marketing is easy, however, from the lower sales management positions.

The sales experience gained and training program taken from almost any large firm are highly transferable. As is often the case, it is easier to transfer from larger to smaller firms than vice versa. Sales representatives rarely cross the line, however, between industrial and consumer packaged products.

Many salespeople use their sales experience to start their own ventures.

*Depending on performance.

Some Employers

Pharmaceutical and Chemical

Abbot Laboratories (North Chicago, Illinois)
Becton Dickinson (Paramus, New Jersey)
Eli Lilly (Indianapolis, Indiana)
Monsanto (St. Louis, Missouri)
Pennwalt (Philadelphia, Pennsylvania)
Union Carbide (New York, New York)

Electronic and Electrical

Automatix (Redmond, Washington)
Datapoint (San Antonio, Texas)
Genrad (Concord, Massachusetts)
Harris Corp. (Melbourne, Florida)
Hewlett-Packard Co. (Palo Alto, California)
IBM (Armonk, New York)
Intel (Santa Clara, California)
Lincoln Electric (Cleveland, Ohio)
Mostek (Carollton, Texas)
Perkin-Elmer (Norwalk, Connecticut)
Teradyne (Boston, Massachusetts)
Texas Instruments (Dallas, Texas)
Western Electric (New York, New York)
Scientific-Atlanta (Atlanta, Georgia)

Paper and Printing

R. R. Donnelly (New York, New York)
International Paper (New York, New York)
Scott Paper (Philadelphia, Pennsylvania)
Union Camp (Wayne, New Jersey)

Consumer Packaged Products

General Foods (White Plains, New York)
General Mills (Minneapolis, Minnesota)
Johnson & Johnson (New Brunswick, New Jersey)
Procter & Gamble (Cincinnati, Ohio)

Additional Information

While technical and industrial sales have traditionally been a "man's world," women have rapidly gained entry in recent years and now comprise 12.8 percent of the 1.3 million salespeople representing U.S. manufacturing companies and wholesalers. The barriers to women are reportedly significant, but not insurmountable. Most important traits are tolerance, technical expertise, and a sense of humor.

Women are more welcomed in consumer packaged product sales, though they experience some of the same difficulties.

Sources of Additional Information

KANTER, ROSABETH MOSS and STEIN, BARRY A. "Birth of a Saleswoman," *Across the Board*, June 1979.

BROWN, RONALD. From Selling to Managing, American Management Association, New York 1968.

MENZIES, HUGH D. "The New Life of a Salesman," *Fortune,* August 11, 1980.

CAREY, JAMES F. "Sales Supervisor: Coach or Adversary?" *S.A.M. Advanced Management Journal*, Spring 1979.

NICHOLS-MANNING, CATHY. "Sales to Marketing: The Crucial Transition," *Management Review*, July 1978.

SALES: INDUSTRIAL

Education (degrees)	BA	MBA	PhD
Experience required (yrs)	None	1-3	3+
Location	Urban	Rural	Regional / Travel
Compensation ($/yr)	< $25K	$25-30K	$30-35K / >$35K
Work involvement (hrs/wk)	< 50	50-60	> 60
Pace	Relaxed	Medium	Frenetic
Career path (a la Driver)	Spiral	Steady	Linear
Interpersonal style	Loner	Moderate	Outgoing
Cognitive style	Sequential Rules Details	Mixed Principles Systems	Random Free form Big picture
Variety (preference for)	No change Ordered	Occasional Change	Ambiguous Changing

Job Description:

MBAs with prior sales experience generally begin in sales management. Those without prior experience may begin as salesmen and then progress into management after a year or so. The duties of Sales Managers include study in developing and managing of sales training programs, sales forecasting, determining pricing policy, analyzing market trends, determining the structure of the sales department, hiring sales representatives, and performing customer service.

Skills

The key skills required are communication skills, motivational ability, empathy, and a goal orientation.

Compensation

The structure and level of industrial sales compensation varies widely, but a few generalizations are possible:

A portion of compensation is normally tied to sales results—either a commission or a bonus.

The more complicated and technologically sophisticated a product is, the less compensation will be tied to sales results.

Distributor sales forces will be paid more on a commission basis than a direct sales force.

Sales can be *very* lucrative.

Perks include company cars, free meals, expense accounts, and lots of travel. The 1981 Harvard Business School graduate compensation (in industrial sales) ranged from $18,000 to $72,000 with a mean of $37,480.

Career Paths

The potential for industrial sales positions is a function of the company and industry itself. Industrial sales experience is very transferable within its specialized field. The possibilities, however, are slim that an individual sales job will open up new job avenues or functional areas.

Practically all sales management organizations are divided geographically, with each succeeding management position increasing in size and scope. A typical sales career path would be:

Sales Representative
District Manager
Regional Manager
Zone Manager
National Sales Manager
Vice-President of Marketing and Sales
Chief Operating Officer of Marketing and Sales

In reality, job advancement in most firms is effectively limited to the National Sales Manager level. We have failed to uncover a single company that described sales as its critical function. (In many firms, however, such as IBM, sales experience was seen as a prerequisite to a managerial position.)

Employers

Pharmaceutical and Chemical

Abbot Laboratories (North Chicago, Illinois)
Becton Dickinson (Paramus, New Jersey)
Eli Lilly (Indianapolis, Indiana)
Monsanto (St. Louis, Missouri)
Pennwalt (Philadelphia, Pennsylvania)
Union Carbide (New York, New York)

Electronic and Electrical

Analog Devices (Norwood, Massachusetts)
Automatix (Redmond, Washington)
Benthos (Falmouth, Massachusetts)
Datapoint (San Antonio, Texas)
Genrad (Concord, Massachusetts)
Harris Corp. (Melbourne, Florida)
Hewlett-Packard Co. (Palo Alto, California)
IBM (Armonk, New York)
Intel (Santa Clara, California)
Lincoln Electric (Cleveland, Ohio)
Mostek (Carollton, Texas)
Perkin-Elmer (Norwalk, Connecticut)
Teradyne (Boston, Massachusetts)
Texas Instruments (Dallas, Texas)
Western Electric (New York, New York)

Paper and Printing

R. R. Donnelly (New York, New York)
International Paper (New York, New York)
Scott Paper (Philadelphia, Pennsylvania)
Union Camp (Wayne, New Jersey)

Miscellaneous

Southern Pacific Co. (San Francisco, California)

Sources of Additional Information

Refer to p. 83.

Unit 2

Industry Reports

15 ADVERTISING

Education (degrees)	BA	MBA	PhD
Experience required (yrs)	None	1-3	3+
Location	Urban	Rural	Regional / Travel
Compensation ($/yr)	< $25K	$25-30K	$30-35K / >$35K
Work involvement (hrs/wk)	< 50	50-60	> 60
Pace	Relaxed	Medium	Frenetic
Career path (a la Driver)	Spiral	Steady	Linear
Interpersonal style	Loner	Moderate	Outgoing
Cognitive style	Sequential Rules Details	Mixed Principles Systems	Random Free form Big picture
Variety (preference for)	No change Ordered	Occasional Change	Ambiguous Changing

Job Description/Typical Day

MBAs usually begin in advertising as Assistant Account Executives working under the direction of an Account Executive (A/E). The Assistant A/E is involved in:

1. Learning the business—which involves exposure to strategic planning, advertising media, the creative process, production, and research.
2. Budgeting—which involves assuming control of the budget and reporting its status to the A/E and the client.
3. Competitive reporting—which involves monitoring the marketplace, including competitors' copy and spending, and keeps the client apprised of key developments.
4. Proposing and developing marketing recommendations to the client.
5. Internal management—which involves making sure that the process of getting ideas to market goes smoothly, which includes coordinating legal, creative, broadcast, and traffic personnel.

Assistant A/Es and A/Es spend most of their time implementing advertising campaigns. One aspect of an advertising career is the amount of variety and change it provides. A time breakdown for an A/E would generally be as follows (an Assistant A/E spends more time on the detail tasks):

Amount of Time	Tasks
25%	Helping creative, media, and research specialists make changes and meet deadlines expected by clients
20%	Monitoring how media are being purchased, compared to budget
20%	Analyzing advertising research
15%	Strategic and marketing planning
5%	Sales promotions and packaging for client
5%	Sales
5%	Research/product development for client
5%	Miscellaneous

Pressures are extreme and working hours are long and unpredictable. Advertising is a very competitive field, and there is little job security. The loss of a large account can mean the firing or laying off of everyone who worked on an account, including the account executive.[1]

Skills

An A/E requires organizational and conceptual ability, excellent communication and presentation skills, management ability, enthusiasm, creativity, patience, and the ability to work long hours under pressure.

[1]*Careers Encyclopedia,* Dow Jones-Irwin, Homewood, Illinois, 1980. p.9.

Compensation

The salary range for 1981 Darden (UVA) graduate students in advertising was $21,000 to $25,000, with a mean of $23,000. A 1981 *Advertising Age* survey put the 1980 average salary range for an A/E between $20,000 and $35,000.[2]

Typical Career Path

A typical career path would be Assistant Account Executive for 12 to 18 months, then Account Executive for 3 to 5 years (responsible for daily operations of one or more client accounts), followed by Account Supervisor (supervises A/Es and sets strategic objectives) for 5 to 8 years, to Management Supervisor for 10 years (responsible for hiring and firing, salaries, and budget).

There is substantial job switching from agency to agency, agency to client, and client to agency. Few transfer, however, from account management to the creative side, or vice versa. A/Es can travel frequently for their clients, but they are not required to transfer to different cities for promotion.

Some Employers

Ad agencies exist in many cities, but the heaviest concentration is in New York, Los Angeles, and Chicago.

N.W. Ayers (New York, New York)
Ted Bates (New York, New York)
BBDO International (New York, New York)
Benton & Bowles (New York, New York)
Leo Burnett (Chicago, Illinois)
Dancer Fitzgerald Sample (New York, New York)
D'Arcy MacManus & Masius (Bloomfield Hills, Michigan)
Doyle, Dane, Bernbach (New York, New York)
Foot, Cone, Belding (Chicago, Illinois)
Grey Advertising (New York, New York)
McCann-Erickson (New York, New York)
Ogilvy & Mather, International (New York, New York)
SSC&B (New York, New York)
J. Walter Thompson (New York, New York)
Young & Rubicam (New York, New York)

[2]"Agency Salaries Lag," *Advertising Age*, May 4, 1981, p.3.

Additional Information

Fifty-four percent of graduate students who go into advertising are hired from campus interviews. Prestige schools appear to have less of an advantage in this field than in others. Forty-four percent of people who enter advertising today are women. Eighty-eight percent of graduate students who enter advertising enter account management.

Sources of Additional Information

The Standard Directory of Advertising Agencies-The Agency Red Book, National Register Publishing Company, Wilmette, Illinois.

16 AEROSPACE

Education (degrees)	BA	MBA	PhD
Experience required (yrs)	None	1-3	3+
Location	Urban	Rural	Regional / Travel
Compensation ($/yr)	< $25K	$25-30K	$30-35K / >$35K
Work involvement (hrs/wk)	< 50	50-60	> 60
Pace	Relaxed	Medium	Frenetic
Career path (a la Driver)	Spiral	Steady	Linear
Interpersonal style	Loner	Moderate	Outgoing
Cognitive style	Sequential Rules Details	Mixed Principles Systems	Random Free form Big picture
Variety (preference for)	No change Ordered	Occasional Change	Ambiguous Changing

INTRODUCTION

The aerospace field encompasses many different businesses, including makers of military and commercial aircraft, space vehicles, satellites, ground support equipment, communications equipment, and so on. There are several major airframe manufacturers and a huge number of vendors and subcontractors that serve the industry.

The number of MBAs recruited by even the largest aerospace firms constitutes only a miniscule portion of their total work force. (Boeing recruits 20 to 25 MBAs per year while employing 90,000 people; McDonnell Douglas does not recruit MBAs at all.) However, MBA jobs that exist (or are sought out by MBAs) seem to have good long-term growth opportunities. The positions formally earmarked for MBAs are generally in finance; MBAs may also find a niche in engineering management, technical program/project management, manufacturing management, marketing, materials buyer training, or personnel. Requirements vary greatly among firms, but many openings require (or strongly favor) a technical background and some pertinent work experience. This is due to the technical nature of the products and the consequent engineering orientation of most of the firms' employees.

Job Description/Typical Day

The following is a job description for a Financial Analyst position from one of the industry's large employers.

Aerospace Financial Analyst

1. Organizational relationship: The Financial Planning Analyst-Aerospace reports to the Director of Business Analysis-Aerospace. The position involves contact with the Vice-President and Controller, the Director of Business Analysis-Aerospace, the Managers of Business Analysis-Aerospace, and divisional financial analysis personnel.
2. Basic functions:
    a. Provide necessary analytical and administrative support to the Director of Business Analysis-Aerospace.
    b. Develop financial reports and prepare special studies as directed by the Director of Business Analysis.
    c. Substitute for Manager of Financial Analysis-Aerospace in the event of a position vacancy.
3. Duties and responsibilities:
    a. Assist in reporting of financial performance goals.
    b. Develop and complete consolidated aerospace operating reports.
    c. Review and critique operating plans and forecasts.
    d. Prepare written and oral presentations to the Corporate Controller and senior management concerning attainment of performance goals.
    e. Prepare product line and contract performance analyses.
    f. Identify risk characteristics of particular contracts.
    g. Participate in corporate task forces when assigned by the Director of Business Analysis-Aerospace.

There are also, in addition to the normal responsibilities, numerous assign-ments of a special nature. Three of these are:

1. Establishing a formal reporting system for the aerospace companies on a monthly and quarterly basis
2. Participating in a management task force to review productivity at the four aerospace divisions
3. Preparing a special analysis to determine the break-even point between a cost-plus and fixed-price contract

Life-styles and routines differ among firms. Travel may be frequent. Promo-tions are often occasioned by transfers to different divisions or locations.

Skills

Some useful personal qualities are good communication skills, motivation, strong career interest in the industry (the firms want "Lifers"), integrity, potential for advancement to larger or different responsibilities, and "fit" with the particu-lar organization. Different firms will value each of these differently.

Compensation

Of course, salaries depend on degrees held, background experience, and the specific position and firm being entered. Salaries quoted (*MBA Executive Industry Report)* in 1978 ranged from $15,000 to $26,000, or roughly 73 percent of the average wages paid entry-level consultants. The Harvard Business School *1981 Numbers Book* indicated a mean starting salary in the Transportation Equipment category of $34,600, while the mean for the entire class was $37,480. The larger firms offer complete standard benefit packages, comparable to those in other industries' major firms.

Typical Career Paths

The few MBAs in the industry are highly visible and are monitored by upper management, often one-to-one by a corporate officer. This in itself presents challenges and opportunities. Many MBAs are "fast-tracked," although that may not involve as rapid a progression in responsibilities or compensation as it might in other industries. Career decisions may involve whether to remain in a technical specialty or enter supervisory functions. Entering MBAs often rotate among various functions and from staff to line.

Larger firms are interested in internal development of upper management through nurturance of long-term relationships. As a result, MBAs typically spend a considerable portion of their careers at the division level, changing positions every three to five years, before moving into a corporate spot. While the faster pace of smaller aerospace firms may appeal to some MBAs, two to four years of initial experience in a large firm is considered a definite advantage.

Sales and marketing experience in other areas generally does not transfer to the aerospace industry, unless government experience or specifically similar types of capital equipment are involved. Boeing and Lockheed hire from within the industry for finance, personnel, and manufacturing positions, while Rockwell and United Technologies look outside.

An example of a successful career path is that of T. A. Wilson, Chief Executive Officer (CEO) of Boeing. With a Master of Science degree from Caltech, he began at Boeing as Assistant Chief to Technical Staffs, was promoted to Manager of Project Engineering, Manager of the Minuteman Program, and then Vice-President of Operations and Planning, followed by a series of other top-level VP positions. As we have noted, of the CEOs of the top five aerospace employers, only Ray Anderson of Lockheed is an MBA.

Some Employers

While the industry projects 7 percent growth in total employment, there is large concern for the fate of the airline segment of the industry, if not defense contracting. (Note "Additional Information.") Airlines projected a recession in 1981 and 1982 (before knowing about the PATCO strike), and the cyclical nature of supplying them is exacerbated by European and Japanese competitive threats. The five largest domestic employers are:

Boeing (Seattle, Washington)
Lockheed (Burbank, California)
McDonnell Douglas (Long Beach, California)
Rockwell International (Pittsburgh, Pennsylvania)
United Technologies (Hartford, Connecticut)

Boeing hires 20 to 25 MBAs annually, Lockheed 12 to 14, and Rockwell about 10. Other (primarily large) firms potentially employing MBAs are the following:

AVCO Corporation (Greenwich, Connecticut)
Beech (Wichita, Kansas)
Bendix (Southfield, Michigan)
Cessna (Wichita, Kansas)
Fairchild (Germantown, Maryland)
Ford Aerospace & Communications (Detroit, Michigan)
General Dynamics (St. Louis, Missouri)
Grumman (Bethpage, New York)
Hughes Aircraft (Culver City, California)
Martin Marietta (Bethesda, Maryland)
Mitsubishi (Tokyo, Japan)
NASA (Houston, Texas)
Northrop (Los Angeles, California)
Piper (Lock Haven, Pennsylvania)
Raytheon (Lexington, Massachusetts)

Rohr Industries (Chula Vista, California)
Textron/Bell Helicopter (Fort Worth, Texas)
TRW (Cleveland, Ohio)

Additional Information

The absence of institutionalized MBA recruiting makes job seeking and personal contact essential. Showing an employer a strong interest in and knowledge of a specific area where your talents are of value is a key factor for success in seeking any specific position.

The industry has a history of cutbacks, which have sometimes been drastic. In 1971 over 100,000 engineers were laid off. The industry is highly dependent on federal outlay. Aerospace is the United States's second largest export industry (after agriculture), at $12 billion in 1980.

Sources of Additional Information

Aerospace Industries Association (AIA)
American Institute of Aeronautics & Astronautics (AIAA)
Aviation Week & Space Technology
Business and Commercial Aviation
World Aviation Directory: Aviation/Aerospace Companies & Officials

17 AGRIBUSINESS

INTRODUCTION

Agribusiness jobs range from the purely technical (trading) to the purely operational (agricultural production). Between those two extremes, jobs for MBAs are available administering and developing public policy, performing financial and operational analysis, supervising control functions (e.g., variance analysis, cost control), developing and implementing distribution and marketing strategies, and managing human resources (an especially challenging task when different nations and cultures are involved).

One's life-style in agribusiness depends, of course, on the particular area one enters. Most production careers, be they international or domestic, provide adventure and require an independent individual with a high tolerance for ambiguity. Since adversities often arise from powers over which the MBA has no control (the weather and government), one must be able to deal with short-term setbacks and improvise to create success in many situations.

We shall review three areas of potential for MBAs in agribusiness: opportunities in the public sector, commodity trading, and national/ international agriculture corporations.

AGRIBUSINESS: PUBLIC SECTOR

Education (degrees)	BA	MBA	PhD
Experience required (yrs)	None	1-3	3+
Location	Urban	Rural	Regional / Travel
Compensation ($/yr)	< $25K	$25-30K	$30-35K / >$35K
Work involvement (hrs/wk)	< 50	50-60	> 60
Pace	Relaxed	Medium	Frenetic
Career path (a la Driver)	Spiral	Steady	Linear
Interpersonal style	Loner	Moderate	Outgoing
Cognitive style	Sequential Rules Details	Mixed Principles Systems	Random Free form Big picture
Variety (preference for)	No change Ordered	Occasional Change	Ambiguous Changing

Job Description/Typical Day

In the public sector, the Department of Agriculture (USDA) offers several career opportunities fairly free of the traditional bureaucratic trappings associated with government work. USDA's Foreign Agricultural Service tends in general to attract higher-level recruits than other agencies. Two areas of particular interest to MBAs would be the Agricultural Attache Service and the Cooperator Program.

Overseas assignments in the Attache Service are usually for two years at a time but are tending to run longer as budget considerations come into play. Plum assignments such as European markets are reserved for long-tenured, politically astute managers, so be prepared for less desirable posts initially. Work overseas involves facilitating U.S. agribusiness export activities, plus data gathering. There is good opportunity for contact with both U.S. and foreign agribusiness at a fairly high level. The Cooperator Program assists U.S. companies in their export efforts; this program is a good way to make contact with agribusiness firms. One caution: women are not particularly welcomed (not because of the Department's bias, but because of their limited access to critical information sources in "less enlightened" countries).

If you are interested in developing countries, the Office of International Cooperation and Development is a good place to get in on the ground floor of joint efforts between U.S. companies and developing country governments. Exciting trends and opportunities are taking shape in agreements being negotiated with several African and Middle Eastern countries.

Skills

The most important skill required in the Attache Service is analytical ability, since initial duties involve analysis of international commodity supply and demand situations. Ability to cope with number-crunching and data-gathering activities is important, as is an ability to deal with the frustrations of having to rely on inexact or incomplete information and dependence on other more bureaucratic sources for information. For positions involving contract negotiations with developing countries, interpersonal skills are the most useful. Good credentials are very impressive; doctoral degrees are best but MBAs are okay.

Compensation

In the public sector, the entry-level salary ranges between $20,000 and $23,000 but depends heavily on previous salary levels. Office of Personnel determines grade eligibility and uses salary history as major criteria. Overseas benefits usually include housing, utilities, and yearly transportation home for expatriates.

Typical Career Paths

USDA - Foreign Agricultural Service. The MBA would begin with two years as an analyst, with frequent rotation between different commodity areas. He or she would receive extensive Attache Service training, including language at

Foreign Service Institute if necessary. Then two years overseas, back for two years of home assignment, and out again. Note: wrong political persuasion or lack of political savvy can result in sidetracking to more mundane, bureaucratic positions. All USDA positions follow the general government promotion plan— only one promotion a year and a legislatively imposed ceiling of about $50,000. Many MBAs take Assistant-to positions or come in, after many years of outside work, as Assistant Secretary (who has Assistant-to type positions to fill) or in upper (politically appointed) management levels in a specific agency. There is increasing interest, however, in getting higher-caliber people in line positions.

Some Employers

Asian Development Bank (Manila, The Phillipines)
European Development Bank (Luxembourg)
United Nations: FAO, UNIDQ, UNESCO (Rome, Italy)
U.S. Department of Agriculture (Washington, D.C.)
World Bank (Washington, D.C.)

Sources of Additional Information

Agricultural Outlook
Agriculture Abroad

AGRIBUSINESS: COMMODITY TRADING

	BA	MBA	PhD
Education (degrees)	BA	MBA	PhD
Experience required (yrs)	None	1-3	3+
Location	Urban	Rural	Regional / Travel
Compensation ($/yr)	< $25K	$25-30K	$30-35K / >$35K
Work involvement (hrs/wk)	< 50	50-60	> 60
Pace	Relaxed	Medium	Frenetic
Career path (a la Driver)	Spiral	Steady	Linear
Interpersonal style	Loner	Moderate	Outgoing
Cognitive style	Sequential Rules Details	Mixed Principles Systems	Random Free form Big picture
Variety (preference for)	No change Ordered	Occasional Change	Ambiguous Changing

Job Description/Typical Day

Commodity trading is high-pressure, intense, action-oriented work. (Watching the Chicago Board of Trade pit is like watching a huge brawl—people have actually been severely hurt during some of the more physical trading sessions.) If you like lots of physical action—as opposed to desk work and office politicking—this is the place for you. (Several years ago there was a female trader at CBT—she liked the work but had to ask men to call out some of her bids since she couldn't yell loudly enough to be heard!)

Skills

Commodity Traders require analytical ability, aggressiveness, and the ability to cope with fast pace and high pressure.

Compensation

Commodity Traders start off at a fairly low salary level but a tripling of salary in a year is not unusual, depending upon ability. Seats on the CBT are limited and fairly expensive, so the graduate needs to start with an established trading firm.

Typical Career Paths

The career path of a trader is flat like that of the professions. Career progression comes through increased responsibility and better trading products.

Some Employers

Clayton Brokerage Co. (St. Louis, Missouri)
Lind-Waldock (Chicago, Illinois)
Index Futures Group, Inc. (Chicago, Illinois)
Minneapolis Grain Exchange (Minneapolis, Minnesota)

Sources of Additional Information

See the following periodicals:

Journal of Agricultural Economics
Futures

AGRIBUSINESS: CORPORATE AGRICULTURE

	BA	MBA	PhD
Education (degrees)	BA	MBA	PhD
Experience required (yrs)	None	1-3	3+
Location	Urban	Rural	Regional / Travel
Compensation ($/yr)	< $25K	$25-30K	$30-35K / >$35K
Work involvement (hrs/wk)	< 50	50-60	> 60
Pace	Relaxed	Medium	Frenetic
Career path (a la Driver)	Spiral	Steady	Linear
Interpersonal style	Loner	Moderate	Outgoing
Cognitive style	Sequential Rules Details	Mixed Principles Systems	Random Free form Big picture
Variety (preference for)	No change Ordered	Occasional Change	Ambiguous Changing

Job Description/Typical Day

Traditionally there have been three levels of commitment in international agricultural corporations—corporate staff, project expatriates, and project nationals—and three functional career streams—field (Agriculturists), factory (Engineers), and finance (Accountants), with parallel streams. The Agriculturists appear to be on a slightly faster track.

These firms do not employ large numbers of MBAs, but over the last five years there have been a series of takeovers and management shakeups; top managements now contain more finance and fewer agricultural people. This may indicate that the field is more receptive to MBA talents.

One important characteristic of agribusiness companies that may have significant life-style implications is the fact that many major firms are not located in major urban centers. For example, Cargill, the number-one grain trader and world's largest agribusiness firm ($11.3 billion in 1979 sales) has its headquarters in Minnetonka, Minnesota, and Archer Daniels Midland is headquartered in Decatur, Illinois.

Typical Career Paths

An entry-level employee would be posted to an overseas project for four to five years as a cadet and then returned to headquarters for two years. The next position would be overseas as a Supervisor, followed by two years at headquarters and then five or more years overseas as a Department Manager. Senior positions as Project Manager, Project Appraiser, and Visiting Agriculturist/Engineer are then available.

For a job with a company such as Castle & Cooke (Honolulu, Hawaii), the career path is as follows:

Job	Usual Tenure	Location
Financial Analyst	1 year	Latin America/Philippines
Operations Manager	3 years	"
Controller/Assistant General Manager	2 years	"
General Manager	3 years	"
Division Vice-President		United States

Some Employers

Anderson Clayton (Houston, Texas)
Archer Daniels Midland (Decatur, Illinois)
Cargill (Minnetonka, Minnesota)
Castle & Cooke (Honolulu, Hawaii)
Consolidated Food Corp. (Chicago, Illinois)
Continental (New York, New York)

CPC International Inc. (Englewood Cliffs, New Jersey)
Esmark (Chicago, Illinois)
General Foods (White Plains, New York)
General Mills (Minneapolis, Minnesota)
Iowa Beef Processors (Dakota City, Nebraska)
Kraft (Glenview, Illinois)
Nestlé (Vevey, Switzerland; White Plains, New York)
Ralston Purina (St. Louis, Missouri)
Staley (Decatur, Illinois)
United Brands (New York, New York)

Sources of Additional Information

Farm Journal
Forest Industry

18 AIRLINES

Education (degrees)	BA	MBA	PhD
Experience required (yrs)	None	1-3	3+
Location	Urban	Rural	Regional / Travel
Compensation ($/yr)	< $25K	$25-30K	$30-35K / >$35K
Work involvement (hrs/wk)	< 50	50-60	> 60
Pace	Relaxed	Medium	Frenetic
Career path (a la Driver)	Spiral	Steady	Linear
Interpersonal style	Loner	Moderate	Outgoing
Cognitive style	Sequential Rules Details	Mixed Principles Systems	Random Free form Big picture
Variety (preference for)	No change Ordered	Occasional Change	Ambiguous Changing

Job Description/Typical Day

Activities of the entry-level MBA are typically in Staff Analyst positions in marketing, finance/control, or occasionally in operations. The highly competitive nature of this industry dictates that pricing implications, cost monitoring, and competitive analysis are a vital part of any position's responsibilities.
Typical position descriptions are the following:

Marketing Analyst

Write market plans for particular flights, cities, or regions
Provide recommendations for pricing and fare structures
Perform competitor and industry analysis
Develop schedules and traffic data
Forecast passenger loads and requirements

Financial Analyst

Analyze capital expenditure proposals, cost savings, return-on-investment analysis
Forecast future profitability, often using computer models
Develop and measure operating budgets, cost control systems
Generate special reports, for example, comparison with competitors
Do impact studies on profits due to fleet competition, traffic load, and changes of routine

Operations Analyst

Develop and run resource allocation models
Develop optimized crew staffing plans
Analyze fleet efficiency, systems optimization

These positions are generally located in metropolitan areas; some airlines require periodic relocations. Work is usually done at headquarters with a strong staff orientation. Working hours are fairly regular, with occasional periods of overtime during budget or appropriation sessions.

Skills and Credentials

Entry-level MBAs should possess strong analytical skills and be able to identify problems and their implications and impacts. Communications and persuasion skills are crucial: the staff nature of the positions requires persuading others in the organization of your conclusions. Persons considering this industry should be task oriented and feel comfortable pushing numbers, working against deadlines, and being required to produce concrete results.

Compensation

Examples of starting 1980 salaries (hiring airline in parentheses) are:

Financial/Marketing Analyst	$15,000-25,000 (American Airlines)
Financial Analyst, Customer, Service,	
Personnel Manager	$18,000 (Texas International)
Senior Financial Analyst	$20,000 (TWA)

It should be noted that in addition to these salaries, there are the normal fringes and a very substantial benefit: travel at highly reduced rates, as low as 10 percent of the normal fare.

The following table indicates the salary levels being paid at the top.

	Chief Executive Officer	Chief Financial Officer	Comptroller	Treasurer
Salary + bonus (85 percent of carriers)	$216,000	$105,000	$58,000	$57,000
Salary, no bonus	94,000	58,000	41,000	39,000

Note that bonus-paying carriers reward the CEO at a much higher rate and that there tends to be salary compression at the CFO position and below in the nonbonus-paying carriers. For further information, consult *Executive Compensation*, published by the Financial Executive Institute (New York).

Career Paths

Future potential is good for *some* airlines (i.e., the stable "biggies" and growing small companies). Among the international carriers, the large, viable firms, such as TWA, are probably here to stay and provide reasonable potential. Others, such as Pan Am, have grave problems at the present just trying to survive and, hence, may offer only limited, high-risk prospects. For the domestic carriers, deregulation has brought about an environment of great change and intensive competition. Many predict that in five to ten years there will be only two national airlines and a host of regional ones, meaning that some will be growing and quite a few will shrink. It is, therefore, crucial to a new entry's prospects that he or she select the "right" airline.

A good track record and/or specific skills should ensure reasonable prospects of transferability between airlines, although these may be limited over the immediate term by the generally tight state of the industry's employment. Personal contacts and reputation are important in this industry.

The larger airlines tend to use the usual MBA executive/analyst/management training posts. Smaller airlines tend to be distinctly entrepreneurial and entry positions may be more comprehensive and offer greater, earlier responsibility. Promotion can be rapid in smaller, growing airlines that tend to be meritocratic, while the usual hierarchical promotion routes prevail in the larger carriers. Intermediate potential: Vice-President of Marketing/Operations/Finance in all companies.

Employers

The industry is segmented roughly as follows:

Trunks, Majors

TWA (New York, New York)
Eastern Airlines (Miami, Florida)
Pan American (New York, New York)
Delta Air Lines (Atlanta, Georgia)
American Airlines (Dallas, Texas)

"Upstarts/No Frills"

New York Airlines (Flushing, New York)
Midway Air Lines (Chicago, Illinois)
People Express Airlines (Newark, New Jersey)

Supplemental/Charter

Capitol Air (Smyrna, Tennessee)
TransAmerica Airlines (Oakland, California)
World Airways (Oakland, California)

Regionals

US Air Inc. (Washington, D.C.)
Piedmont Aviation (Winston-Salem, North Carolina)
Air Florida (Miami, Florida)

Commuter

Pilgrim Aviation & Airlines (Groton, Connecticut)
Ransome Airlines (Richmond, Virginia)

Air Freight

Federal Express (Memphis, Tennessee)
Emery Air Freight (Wilton, Connecticut)

Additional Information

Industry trends.   Due to deregulation, the number of carriers (now 66) doubled from 1978 to 1981. Regional carriers have captured share from trunk carriers and now have a 12 percent share of the domestic market compared with 8 percent before deregulation. Revenue growth for regionals was estimated at 20 percent per year between 1977 and 1982 compared with 15 percent for the trunk carriers.

Employment trends.   Despite a revenue increase of 24 percent for 1980 over 1979, domestic airlines furloughed 15,000 employees in 1980. Continental hit its officers with a 10 percent across-the-board pay cut in August 1981. Deregulation, however, has also provided a hidden, albeit short-term, benefit to some carriers with the appropriate schedules and route structure: the ability to reduce the number of flights and to increase load factors. This, combined with the ability to set fares flexibly according to demand, will provide carriers with somewhat greater opportunities for financial health than the statistics might otherwise indicate.

Sources of Additional Information

Air Transport World
Transportation Journal

19 COLLEGE ADMINISTRATION AND HIGHER EDUCATION

Education (degrees)	BA	MBA	PhD
Experience required (yrs)	None	1-3	3+
Location	Urban	Rural	Regional / Travel
Compensation ($/yr)	$< $25K$	$25-30K	$30-35K / $>$35K
Work involvement (hrs/wk)	< 50	50-60	> 60
Pace	Relaxed	Medium	Frenetic
Career path (a la Driver)	Spiral	Steady	Linear
Interpersonal style	Loner	Moderate	Outgoing
Cognitive style	Sequential Rules Details	Mixed Principles Systems	Random Free form Big picture
Variety (preference for)	No change Ordered	Occasional Change	Ambiguous Changing

INTRODUCTION

In College Administration, people holding a business degree usually enter job positions that deal with teaching, administrative matters, or both. Requirements range from a BA plus five years of experience in administration, through an MBA or CPA, to an Ed.D., DBA, or Ph.D.

The major skills required in all these positions—as portrayed in job descriptions—are organizational, managerial, interpersonal, and financial. In the case of teaching positions, substantive knowledge and expertise in the subject matter are also required. The three areas described next encompass these most common areas within, as for example, a business school setting.

ACADEMIC OPPORTUNITIES

Job Description/Typical Day

Entry-level positions in this area include Research Assistant and Instructor. Research Assistants research and prepare teaching (case) materials. In addition to teaching, Instructors usually continue their postgraduate research. The degree to which "publish or perish" prevails varies with the size and philosophy of the school, but all teachers are encouraged to maintain their expertise through continued research and publication.

Skills

Most teaching positions require an MBA and a DBA, a Ph.D., or its equivalent. The increased competition among academic institutions in recent years has led to a greater emphasis on teachers' academic credentials, which in turn has reduced the transfer from business to the academic scene.

Required skills include expertise in a particular subject matter, excellent written and oral communication skills, organizational ability, and, often, prior teaching experiences.

Compensation

Assistant Professors at major business schools can expect to earn about the average starting MBA salary for that school, but subsequent raises may not keep pace with the rising average MBA starting salaries. Outside (consulting) income is a major source of income that may double or triple the professor's income five to ten years into the career.

Typical Career Paths

The most common career path is to enter the teaching field directly upon receiving an advanced degree. Another option is to work in business first and then enter the teaching profession. Generally, two years is the maximum amount of time that can be spent in business and still allow immediate access to teaching. More than two years out of the academic field usually requires entry into administrative academic positions and, from there, a transfer to teaching.

One progresses within the teaching function from Instructor to Assistant to Associate to Full Professor. For those wishing to branch into administrative duties, further opportunities exist such as Dean and President of the university.

Many professors supplement their teaching and research activities with consulting. The degree to which consulting work is available depends upon the reputation of the school, its interaction with industry, and its proximity to major business centers.

Usually only the top institutions have as much consulting opportunities as faculty would like. A general limitation at many of these schools has been no more than 40 days of consulting per year per professor.

ADMINISTRATIVE OPPORTUNITIES

Job Descriptions/Typical Day

Administrative duties can be divided into fiscal and external affairs. Each of these will be discussed independently.

Fiscal Affairs.   Positions involving fiscal affairs include Business Manager, Budget and Planning Director, Comptroller, Grants Administrator, Registrar, and Director of Financial Aid. Responsibilities in this area are managing financial and business affairs, managing university assets and endowment, facilities planning, data processing and information services, submission and acceptance of grant agreements, and managing student loans.

Skills

The skills and qualifications necessary for these jobs are an MBA or BA and five years of experience in both educational and financial areas, managerial ability, and previous supervisory experience.

External Affairs.   Positions involving external affairs include Resource Development Officer, Recruitment Specialist, Assistant or Director of Career Planning and Placement, Assistant or Director of Admission, Alumni Director, and Assistant or Director of Fundraising and Development.

These positions involve developing and managing relations with students, alumni, donors, and community organizations. Their responsibilities include developing marketing strategies, increasing enrollment, decreasing attrition, and fundraising.

Skills

Qualifications for these positions include an MBA or BA plus one to five years of experience, excellent written and oral communication skills, willingness to travel, and an ability to work with different types of people and organizations.

Compensation

Starting salaries at major business schools tend to be at or below the average starting MBA salaries. These often include medical care and other benefits that can compensate.

Typical Career Paths

There are few set career paths in this area, due to the variety of possible jobs and the degree to which movement is prevalent in those jobs to nonprofit organizations, foundations, and the like.

The following data are based on a 1970 study by Michael R. Ferrari of 760 American college and university presidents (see *Profiles of American College Presidents*, Michigan State University, Division of Research, Graduate School of Business Administration, East Lansing, Michigan, 1970):

> Seventy-five percent had an academic doctorate degree, with Ph.D. most prevalent. Areas of concentration varied, with studies in the humanities the most prevalent.
>
> The majority had spent their full-time careers in educational and professional fields. Eighty-six percent had at some time served as college teachers; 36 percent had taught at the institution they now headed; two-thirds had averaged ten years of full-time academic administrative experience. Average age at assumption of presidency, 45.
>
> The move to the presidency is most often (75 percent) directly from within the field of education — 22 percent from positions as college deans, 11 percent academic vice-presidents, 11 percent department chairpersons, 10 percent college faculty.
>
> Only 2 percent came directly from business, 3 percent from government, 1 percent military, 1 percent foundations.
>
> In two-thirds of the cases, presidents chose careers in higher education, moving through positions of increasing responsibility (i.e., teacher, department administrator, dean, lower-level administration, academic vice-president, then presidency).

Persons with interests in particular academic fields should be aware that due to the difficulty of keeping up with one's field while serving as a dean or president, it may be difficult to return to a top teaching position at a later date.

Employers

U.S. college administrators are facing the challenge of a declining number of college-age persons. Many smaller colleges are consolidating or folding. Some are expanding into continuing education or currently popular graduate programs in areas such as business.

There are various opportunities for those interested in college administration in other countries. Some countries are facing the same problems as the United States with a declining traditional market. Other countries, such as Saudi Arabia, are actively recruiting college personnel from overseas to staff their rapidly growing educational systems.

Nontraditional sources of employment for college administrators include organizations such as General Electric, IBM, and the military. General Electric has a formal program for selected recent college graduates in which the employees rotate in work assignments and take part-time financial courses taught by General Electric employees. Graduates of this program are considered inside and outside of the company to have the equivalent of an MBA.

IBM has a system of company-run schools for employees who appear to have significant managerial potential. This program is full time for a period of months, and instructors are often college faculty on leave. The military also runs colleges such as Annapolis and West Point and maintains educational programs throughout the world for its military personnel stationed overseas.

Sources of Additional Information

> College catalogs and admissions materials
> Ministries of Education in any country

20 COMMERCIAL BANKING

	BA	MBA	PhD
Education (degrees)	BA	MBA	PhD
Experience required (yrs)	None	1-3	3+
Location	Urban	Rural	Regional / Travel
Compensation ($/yr)	< $25K	$25-30K	$30-35K / >$35K
Work involvement (hrs/wk)	< 50	50-60	> 60
Pace	Relaxed	Medium	Frenetic
Career path (a la Driver)	Spiral	Steady	Linear
Interpersonal style	Loner	Moderate	Outgoing
Cognitive style	Sequential Rules Details	Mixed Principles Systems	Random Free form Big picture
Variety (preference for)	No change Ordered	Occasional Change	Ambiguous Changing

INTRODUCTION

There are basically two areas where MBAs find opportunities in commercial banking: lending and operations. The former sells services, the latter delivers them. Consequently, the two areas must work well together. Although banking operations are increasing in status and importance, most MBAs enter the lending side.

Job Description/Typical Day

The Loan Officer is in charge of a portfolio of corporate accounts in one or two industries. He or she may move from industry to industry regularly or may specialize in one or two in depth. The Loan Officer's main function is to offer, extend, or modify credit lines to new and existing clients. This requires careful analysis of the client's needs, ability to repay, and industry. As a Loan Officer, you are, therefore, an analyst and salesperson. You have to sell your analysis and recommendations to the credit committee inside the bank, and you have to sell the terms and conditions of the loans and other bank services to your customer. (This is the toughest part of the job.) Your activities involve teamwork—with credit committee, customers, other banks' officers—as well as independent work to prepare the credit analysis and loan proposals.

Contrary to the popular myth, bankers do not work from 8 to 5. Extra hours are often required, either tying together a critical deal in the office or traveling to other cities on prospect calls. A day is often filled with meetings and phone discussions with customers or other bankers. At times, tasks may become very clerical, but they have to be done.

Banks, by their nature, are conservative and paternalistic. The work climate is secure and supportive rather than competitive and fast track. Bankers are required to play by the rules of the corporate game, including rules of dress and socially acceptable behavior. The lending function is very much a team effort and often requires working as part of a group. The sales part of the job often requires social interaction with clients and potential clients.

Skills

Analytical ability is important for a Lending Officer to understand credit analysis and to package loans and financial deals. Interpersonal skills are required to work within the organization and with clients. A Lending Officer must possess self-confidence and the ability to convince clients of his or her ability to do a good job. Selling skills are necessary, as mentioned, and so is the ability to grasp client requirements quickly and sell ways for your bank to meet those needs. Finally, patience is needed to handle the required paperwork and details.

Compensation

For 1982, starting salaries in domestic lending ranged from $22,000 to $31,000. Eastern banks have traditionally offered higher starting salaries than have Midwestern or Western banks.

Typical Career Paths

Prior to actual "commencement" along a career path, most commercial banks require participation in a training program. This program varies in content from bank to bank, yet frequently it includes exposure to each of the bank's areas. It may last anywhere from 3 to 24 months, depending on the new employee's previous experience and the policies of the bank.

Within both the money center and regional banks, there are three distinct career paths: Lending, Trust, and Operations. The Lending or line position has traditionally represented the most essential and prestigious position in the bank hierarchy. A line officer's credit training enables him or her easily to make a lateral move to a noncredit-related field within the bank, but the converse is not true. Because of the technological revolution in banking, Operations is becoming an important field for the MBA, due to its increasing contribution to profitability. The skills developed in this area are extremely transferable. Finally, the Trust division is relatively small, comprised of officers who are seemingly self-selecting and rarely ever transfer out of their field.

Most banks encourage specialization and discourage transfer. Advancement is fairly predictable, without distinctive "fast tracks." A hard-working MBA can expect to attain a Vice-Presidency (about middle management) within six to ten years of joining the bank. Regarding mobility between banks, it is quite acceptable to transfer from a large bank to a small one, but rarely the other way. If you decide to leave the industry altogether, your financial skills may not be transferable unless a solid track record has been established. A survey of the major money center banks shows that the top three bank officers in almost all cases are "Lifers" (twenty to thirty years service) who rose within various lending divisions.

Some Employers

The two major types of banks are money center and regional banks. Money center banks are located in New York, San Francisco, and Chicago. They rely more on purchased funds and corporate deposits for their base of large corporate clients. Regional banks have considerable influence on a local level, but less on a national and international scale.

Some potential employers are:

Money Center Banks

Bank of America (San Francisco, California)
Bank of New York (New York, New York)
Bankers Trust Co. (New York, New York)
Chase Manhattan Bank (New York, New York)
Chemical Bank (New York, New York)
Citibank (New York, New York)
Continental Illinois National Bank (Chicago, Illinois)
Irving Trust Co. (New York, New York)
Manufacturers Hanover Trust (New York, New York)
Morgan Guaranty Trust (New York, New York)

Regional Banks

Baybanks, Inc. (Cambridge, Massachusetts)
Crocker National Bank (San Francisco, California)
First Chicago (Chicago, Illinois)
First National Bank of Boston (Boston, Massachusetts)
First Wisconsin National Bank (Madison, Wisconsin)
Hartford National Bank (Hartford, Connecticut)
Mellon Bank (Pittsburgh, Pennsylvania)
North Carolina National Bank (Charlotte, North Carolina)
Pittsburgh National Bank (Pittsburgh, Pennsylvania)
Security Pacific National Bank (Los Angeles, California)
Shawmut Bank of Boston, N.A. (Boston, Massachusetts)
Texas Commerce Bank (Houston, Texas)
Wachovia (Winston-Salem, North Carolina)
Wells Fargo Bank (San Francisco, California)

Additional Information

Since the affirmative action legislation of the early 1970s was passed, commercial banking has increasingly opened up to women. In fact, some women feel that the field is one of the best places for them to get ahead in the business world, for performance can be quantified, therefore making it more objective. Furthermore, the field is very visible. Major money center banks, notably Chase, Citibank, and Manufacturers Hanover, have been hiring many women into their training programs (e.g., about 50 percent of Chase trainees are women). Most women tend to go into staff rather than line positions; this could be a subtle form of discrimination, but many women actively choose to remain staff oriented. As indicated by current promotion practices, prospects are quite good for those women aspiring to middle management–level positions (vice-president level). However, prospects for senior management positions are more uncertain—women simply haven't been in the ranks long enough.

Loan Officers spend much of their time putting out fires caused by operations, so when interviewing with a bank, check on the efficiency and capability of its operations department.

Sources of Additional Information

American Banker
The Banker, "The Top 100" (annual June issue)
Business Week, "Annual Scoreboard of 200 Banks"
Forbes, "Annual Banking Issue"
Institutional Investor, "Ranking the 100 Largest Banks"
Magazine of Bank Administration
Moody's Bank & Financial Manual
Savings and Loan News
World Banking, annual survey

21 COMMUNICATIONS

INTRODUCTION

The communications industry broadly defined represents a varied and fast-growing set of career opportunities. In addition to jobs in the traditional functional areas of finance, marketing, and operations, communications offers positions in programming, research and development, and high-tech manufacturing in keeping with the rapid-change context of the '80s. Pressures to deregulate the industry have led to the formation of many new businesses and sub-industries, and technological innovations continue to redefine the operating standards for the industry. Also, customer sophistication and changing demands require an increasingly competitive market orientation. We have included here four sections, two of which (Broadcasting and Cable Television) might have been included in the entertainment unit. Each section deals with a sub-industry involving voice, data, and/or image transmission, though, making it a part of the broader communications industry.

The Broadcasting section looks at careers in entertainment and news broadcasting beginning first with the major networks. The Cable Television section examines opportunities in the fast-growing, somewhat risky cable TV world. The last two sections on Large and Small Telecommunications firms explore jobs in an area that is undergoing fundamental changes. In this twenty-year-old business, fiber optics are making a serious inroad in historically satellite-dominated transmissions, and deregulation has turned the nature of the business from a technologically driven one to an increasingly competitive one. Innovations in technology, like impending abilities to refine signal dispersion to and from geosynchronous satellites positioned 22,300 miles above the equator from 3 degrees of arc to half or a third of that (which will double or triple the potential number of satellites), continue to provide new opportunities for both hopeful and established firms in the industry.

COMMUNICATIONS: BROADCASTING

Education (degrees)	BA	MBA	PhD
Experience required (yrs)	None	1-3	3+
Location	Urban	Rural	Regional / Travel
Compensation ($/yr)	< $25K	$25-30K	$30-35K / >$35K
Work involvement (hrs/wk)	< 50	50-60	> 60
Pace	Relaxed	Medium	Frenetic
Career path (a la Driver)	Spiral	Steady	Linear
Interpersonal style	Loner	Moderate	Outgoing
Cognitive style	Sequential Rules Details	Mixed Principles Systems	Random Free form Big picture
Variety (preference for)	No change Ordered	Occasional Change	Ambiguous Changing

Job Description/Typical Day

Financial planning. Involves financial analysis and budgeting and requires quantitative analytical skills. Related financial experience is often required.

Advertising and promotions. Involves developing and producing internal advertising, mostly for television programs. This position calls for creativity. A lively work environment is traded off against lower salaries.

Sales and marketing positions. Involves selling air time. The tasks of these jobs include marketing of services, sales presentations and promotions, sales planning, media analysis and direct selling. Marketing and sales skills and experience are usually required.

All three of these entry-level areas have a few things in common. Prior related experience is often necessary. There are very few training programs and no set career paths. An MBA entering any of these areas must be prepared to deal with little structure and must be flexible to make his or her own opportunities.

Skills

See Film Industry (pp. 157-159).

Compensation

A survey of 1980 MBAs in the entertainment field indicates that the least satisfying aspect of their job was the starting salary. Most are in the low to mid-20s. (The most satisfying aspect of the job was people/environment.)

Typical Career Paths

There are no established career paths. Advancement depends upon the individual's initiative and the network of contacts he or she develops within the company. The path of an MBA hired in 1975 was

Corporate Planning Analyst
Director of Financial Planning (Radio)
Network Development (Radio)
Vice-President Network (Radio)

Some Employers

ABC and Affiliates (New York, New York)
CBS and Affiliates (New York, New York)
NBC and Affiliates (New York, New York)
Cox Broadcasting Company (Atlanta, Georgia)
Harte-Hanks Communication, Inc. (Richmond, Virginia)
King Broadcasting Company (Seattle, Washington)

Landmark Communications (Norfolk, Virginia)
Taft Broadcasting (Atlanta, Georgia)
Turner Broadcasting (Atlanta, Georgia)
Warner Communications (Burbank, California)

There are also a number of entrepreneurial opportunities in the field. Hundreds of radio stations are sold each year, 10 percent for less than $350,000.

Sources of Additional Information

See Film Industry (pp. 157-159).

COMMUNICATIONS: CABLE TELEVISION

Education (degrees)	BA	MBA	PhD
Experience required (yrs)	None	1-3	3+
Location	Urban	Rural	Regional / Travel
Compensation ($/yr)	< $25K	$25-30K	$30-35K / >$35K
Work involvement (hrs/wk)	< 50	50-60	> 60
Pace	Relaxed	Medium	Frenetic
Career path (a la Driver)	Spiral	Steady	Linear
Interpersonal style	Loner	Moderate	Outgoing
Cognitive style	Sequential Rules Details	Mixed Principles Systems	Random Free form Big picture
Variety (preference for)	No change Ordered	Occasional Change	Ambiguous Changing

INTRODUCTION

As an emerging (reborn) industry, cable television is characterized by high growth, rapid technological change, a dynamic competitive environment, and great uncertainty.

Major players and their roles include

System Operators—Granted exclusive franchises to provide cable television services in a specific area, they build and maintain local CATV plants and distribute programming to local subscribers (e.g., Teleprompter).

Program Producers—Provide program packages to system operations (includes, but is not limited to, films, news, sports events, and other entertainment specials, e.g. HBO—Home Box Office).

Service and Finance Companies—Provide varied consulting and support services (franchising, legal, market research, advertising, organizational development) and financial assistance to operators and producers (e.g., Avco).

Equipment Manufacturers—Supply hardware and related products to operators (e.g., Scientific-Atlanta).

The breadth of integration varies in the industry from large conglomerates to small entrepreneurial operators. There have been several major new entrants recently (e.g., Westinghouse).

As in many areas of communications/entertainment, an MBA has sometimes been seen as a liability. However, many of these firms are now seeing a definite need for MBAs, and hiring has increased. Personal initiative in finding them is still essential, but there are opportunities for the MBA with strong commitment to the industry.

Job Description/Typical Day

In addition to the Financial Analyst position described under Broadcasting, the entry-level positions for cable television are primarily in Staff Marketing or Affiliate Relations positions. Staff Marketing is concerned with internal business operations; Affiliate Relations provide sales and service to customers. The responsibilities of both jobs are to develop, coordinate, and execute marketing strategies; provide consulting to customers; and identify and pursue new business developments.

The routine is varied and the environment is unstructured. The life-style is informal, but there is substantial work-related socializing.

Skills

The major skills needed for these positions are interpersonal skills, flexibility, analytical ability, and the tolerance of ambiguity.

Compensation

In 1980 salaries for entry-level financial or marketing positions were $28,000 to $30,000.

Typical Career Paths

Career paths are uncertain for this fledgling industry. There are opportunities to enter other areas of the entertainment industry, such as production, but the trend has been toward entering rather than leaving cable since this is the fastest-growing segment of the entertainment industry.

Some Employers

System Operators

Acton Corp. (Acton, Massachusetts)
Adams-Russell Co. (Waltham, Massachusetts)
AEL Industries (Lansdale, Pennsylvania)
Canadian Cablesystems (Toronto, Ontario, Canada)
Comcast Corp. (Bala-Cynwyd, Pennsylvania)
Cox Communications (Atlanta, Georgia)
General Electric (Fairfield, Connecticut)
Heritage Communications (Des Moines, Iowa)
Jones Intercable (Englewood, Colorado)
Multimedia Inc. (Greenville, South Carolina)
New York Times (New York, New York)
Rollins, Inc. (Atlanta, Georgia)
Storer Communications (Miami, Florida)
Teleprompter Corp. (New York, New York)
Time-Life (New York, New York)
Times Mirror (Los Angeles, California)
United Artists/Columbia (San Francisco, California)
United Cable Television (Denver, Colorado)
Viacom International (New York, New York)
Warner Communications (New York, New York)
Wometco Enterprises (Miami, Florida)
Wrather Corp. (Beverly Hills, California)

Service and Finance

Avco Embassy Pictures (Los Angeles, California)
Burnup & Sims (Ft. Lauderdale, Florida)
Columbia Pictures (New York, New York)
Walt Disney Productions (Burbank, California)
General Tire & Rubber (Akron, Ohio)

Gulf & Western (New York, New York)
MCA Inc. (Universal City, California)
MGM/UA Entertainment (Culver City, California)
Time, Inc. (New York, New York)
Transamerica Corp. (San Francisco, California)
Turner Broadcasting (Atlanta, Georgia)
20th Century Fox (Los Angeles, California)
Tymshare, Inc. (Cupertino, California)

Program Producers

Home Box Office (New York, New York)
Home Theater Network (Portland, Maine)
The Movie Channel (New York, New York)
Rainbow (Woodbury, New York)
Showtime (New York, New York)

Equipment Manufacturers

Ampex Corp. (Redwood City, California)
Anixter Brothers Inc. (Skokie, Illinois)
Arvin Industries Inc. (Columbus, Indiana)
Augat Inc. (Mansfield, Massachusetts)
Belden Corp. (Geneva, Illinois)
Comtech Data Corp. (Scottsdale, Arizona)
Continental Telecom Inc. (Atlanta, Georgia)
Eastman Kodak (Rochester, New York)
GK Technologies, Inc. (Greenwich, Connecticut)
General Instrument Corp. (Clifton, New Jersey)
GTE (Stamford, Connecticut)
Harris Corp. (Melbourne, Florida)
Insilco Corp. (Meriden, Connecticut)
Microdyne Corp. (Ocala, Florida)
Minnesota Mining & Manufacturing Co. (3M) (St. Paul, Minnesota)
North American Phillips (New York, New York)
Oak Industries (San Diego, California)
RCA (New York, New York)
RMS Electronics Inc. (Bronx, New York)
Scientific-Atlanta (Atlanta, Georgia)
Sony (New York, New York)
Tektronix (Beaverton, Oregon)
Telemation (Salt Lake City, Utah)
Tocom (Irving, Texas)

Sources of Additional Information

CableVision

COMMUNICATIONS: LARGE TELECOMMUNICATIONS FIRMS

Education (degrees)	BA	MBA	PhD
Experience required (yrs)	None	1-3	3+
Location	Urban	Rural	Regional / Travel
Compensation ($/yr)	< $25K	$25-30K	$30-35K / >$35K
Work involvement (hrs/wk)	< 50	50-60	> 60
Pace	Relaxed	Medium	Frenetic
Career path (a la Driver)	Spiral	Steady	Linear
Interpersonal style	Loner	Moderate	Outgoing
Cognitive style	Sequential Rules Details	Mixed Principles Systems	Random Free form Big picture
Variety (preference for)	No change Ordered	Occasional Change	Ambiguous Changing

INTRODUCTION

This industry is characterized by a distinct two-tier structure. On the top are the multinational giants, and on the bottom are the small, rapidly growing, niche-oriented firms.

Job Description/Typical Day

Most of the large companies are technology leaders, with high growth in satellite communications and extreme growth in the high-capacity, data transmission services. Marketing and sales are greatly increasing in importance, as can be seen by the developments at AT&T in recent years.

Many of the companies have so-called Management Development Programs that they staff with top-level MBAs. These fast-track MBAs are moved through several functional areas to gain broad exposure. Other MBAs may be hired as Account Executives, who service the needs of corporate clients within a particular industry. A/Es require extensive training.

The activities of the large firms are similiar to those of the smaller ones—including pricing, promotion, market research, competitor analysis, account/customer contact, strategic planning, and coordination of service functions—but they are performed with greatly increased direction and focus.

The first years out appear to be very structured as in typical larger corporations. Planning areas seem to offer the greatest freedom and visibility in a dimension other than the training program's. Travel can be heavy if one is in sales or marketing, and relocation is expected. Within the first five years, a fast-track MBA may move three or four times.

Skills

Unlike those needed in smaller firms, skills required vary with function chosen. First assignment focuses last year included marketing/sales, production and service operations, project management, and general management. A technical background is becoming increasingly necessary, but is not always required.

Compensation

Salary is low to average (1979 range was $24,000 to $27,000). Evidently training program and wide exposure are meant to compensate.

Typical Career Paths

Special Management Development Program status brings high visibility and high risk. Persons with MDP status can expect to attain District Manager level within three to five years.

If a general management focus is chosen, skills can easily be transferred out of the industry. The greatest value would, of course, be to one of the smaller, second-tier firms, where well-trained general management stock will be at a premium.

Since you would be part of a "fast-track" program, career paths are intentionally tailored to meet the demands of the desired functional concentration. The general management route seems to get all the play in the current recruiting ads.

With the continuing shift toward a marketing orientation, new career paths are also available in national account management (i.e., managing the sales force who call on large corporate accounts).

Some Employers

AT&T Long Lines (New York, New York)

Communications Satellite Company (Washington, D.C.)

Intelsat (Washington, D.C.)

International Telephone and Telegraph (New York, New York)

RCA (New York, New York)

Satellite Business Systems (owned by IBM, Comsat General, Aetna) (McLean, Virginia)

Western Union (Upper Saddle River, New Jersey.)

COMMUNICATIONS: SMALL TELECOMMUNICATIONS FIRMS

Education (degrees)	BA	MBA	PhD
Experience required (yrs)	None	1-3	3+
Location	Urban	Rural	Regional / Travel
Compensation ($/yr)	< $25K	$25-30K	$30-35K / >$35K
Work involvement (hrs/wk)	< 50	50-60	> 60
Pace	Relaxed	Medium	Frenetic
Career path (a la Driver)	Spiral	Steady	Linear
Interpersonal style	Loner	Moderate	Outgoing
Cognitive style	Sequential Rules Details	Mixed Principles Systems	Random Free form Big picture
Variety (preference for)	No change Ordered	Occasional Change	Ambiguous Changing

INTRODUCTION

The smaller, independent telephone and telecommunications companies are technology followers. They compete with the industry giants by finding a market niche and exploiting it. Marketing is the driving force, with operations and R&D existing in a supporting role.

Activities in these companies are similar to those in their larger counterparts, but they are less structured. A larger degree of program planning brings high visibility and access to upper management.

The work environment is relatively unstructured, with moderate to long days, irregular hours, sometimes high pressure, and lots of travel. Because it is a young industry, entrepreneurial attitudes prevail.

Skills

The necessary skills are an ability to deal with ambiguity, sensitivity to political and regulatory events, good presentation skills, willingness and ability to train subordinates and replacements, creative thinking, and an ability to work with little supervision. No technical degrees are required.

Compensation

Starting salaries are greatly affected by prior experience. The average is $30,000 to $31,000. Since performance is stressed, there is a potential for higher than average growth.

Typical Career Paths

Because of the youth of the industry and its high growth and high visibility, career paths depend entirely on performance and initiative. Due to the intense competition among firms, skills are transferable within the data communications field. It is easier to move from large to smaller firms, however, than vice versa.

Some of these firms will fail. This risk creates a highly ambiguous advancement situation. However, the companies that remain will offer significant career growth. Also, some of these firms will expand into electronic mail, data communications, and other communications functions.

Some Employers

Central Telephone and Utilities (Chicago, Illinois)
Continental Telephone (Sycamore, Illinois)
Exxon (through its Qwip and Vydec subsidiaries) (New York, New York)
MCI Telecommunications (Washington, D.C.)
Mid-Continent Telephone (Hudson, Ohio)
Southern Pacific Co. (San Francisco, California)
Sprint Telephone (Stamford, Connecticut)

22 CONSULTING

Education (degrees)	BA	MBA	PhD
Experience required (yrs)	None	1-3	3+
Location	Urban	Rural	Regional / Travel
Compensation ($/yr)	< $25K	$25-30K	$30-35K / >$35K
Work involvement (hrs/wk)	< 50	50-60	> 60
Pace	Relaxed	Medium	Frenetic
Career path (a la Driver)	Spiral	Steady	Linear
Interpersonal style	Loner	Moderate	Outgoing
Cognitive style	Sequential Rules Details	Mixed Principles Systems	Random Free form Big picture
Variety (preference for)	No change Ordered	Occasional Change	Ambiguous Changing

INTRODUCTION

The opportunities for consulting are as varied as the problems and tasks of business. Consulting firms range from partnerships of two or three professionals specializing in a particular industry or function to large corporations employing over a thousand professionals and offering a broad array of services to an international clientele. Despite the firms' differences in size and specialty, some of which will be outlined in the paragraphs that follow, several useful generalizations can be made about the function of the consultant and his or her life-style, compensation, and career development.

Job Description/Typical Day

The major tasks of all Consultants are to determine and/or clarify the client's problem, collect data on the problem, analyze the pertinent data, and develop recommendations. The presentation of these findings and recommendations can take the form of written reports, oral presentations, seminars, or workshops. Some consulting firms will assist with the implementation of their ideas, but often the consultant's task ends with the presentation of findings.

Consulting demands extensive traveling and long hours. On average, a Consultant devotes between 50 and 60 hours per week to work, and an 80-hour workweek may be common during peak periods. Consultants usually work in teams on one or more projects at a time, and a typical project lasts between three and five months.

A typical workweek is as follows:

One day in the office handling administrative work (taking care of correspondence, arranging interviews, etc.)

Two days in the field talking with clients and gathering data

Half a day with team or project manager reviewing documents, monitoring the project's progress, charting strategy for completion of the project

One and a half days analyzing the data and crunching the numbers (during weeks when reports are due, this time would be devoted to writing or producing the report)

Project deadlines, frequent traveling, and the unpredictability of time commitments create a high degree of pressure. The Consultant is often given little direction, and past performance provides little job security. The work pace required by consulting often intrudes upon the individual's personal and social life.

Skills

Conceptual and analytical skills are of primary importance to the Consultant. Before any other work is done, the Consultant must be able to understand a problem, grasp its scope and dimensions, and then determine an approach to solve it. Quantitative analytical skills are needed to process the data collected. Most consulting positions rely heavily on number-crunching skills.

Interpersonal skills are also critical, for the Consultant must deal effectively with all levels of employees in the client company as well as with the members of his or her consulting team. Communicative skills are then necessary to convey information gathered in a productive and nonthreatening manner. (A long-term consulting relationship can easily be broken by a new Consultant who appears condescending or omniscient.) The Consultant also needs organizational skills for he or she is often given little direction and must, therefore, create structure in an otherwise ambiguous situation. As he or she progresses within the firm, the Consultant becomes more of a salesman for his or her services.

The degree of technical skills needed will vary with the type of Consultant and the size of the consulting firm. Large multiservice firms may require little technical skill at the entry level, while small specialty firms will require substantial work experience and advanced technical degrees.

Finally, a Consultant must have stamina to withstand the substantial pressure created by long hours, frequent travel, and constant deadlines.

Compensation

Consulting and investment banking have traditionally been the highest-paying positions for recent MBA graduates. The offers in consulting for the Harvard Business School Class of 1981 ranged from $25,000 to $58,000, while those at UVA's Darden School ranged from $25,000 to $48,000. The salary potential for top-level Consultants can reach well into the six figures. Small, regional firms often pay less than larger international ones. Other employee benefits are low relative to industry, although stock options and profit-sharing plans are offered by many firms. Three weeks of vacation are most often given, although a Consultant's schedule rarely permits this much time off.

Typical Career Paths

Entry-level positions with consulting firms are highly sought after, and consequently most large consulting firms recruit only at the leading four or five business schools. Smaller firms are not so selective yet require greater technical skill and experience from their employees.

The typical entry-level position is as an Associate or Consultant (two to three years). At this level the Consultant is assigned to a project team and is given immediate responsibility in research, analysis, and report writing. He or she is expected to hone these skills while gaining increased exposure to dealing with clients. Next is the Senior Associate or Consultant (one to two years), who is often a Project Manager who directs the junior staff and who is given some selling responsibility. The Manager or Principal (two to four years) is given major sales responsibility. He or she may work on many projects concurrently. This position is essentially a training or proving ground for the Partner's position. The Vice President or Partner is at the top of the consulting hierarchy. He or she is responsible for determining company policy, running a regional office, or heading a particular consulting specialty.

Most firms follow a forced pyramid, or "up-or-out" regime, whereby the Consultant is expected to have developed his or her skills to a certain point by a certain time. At each of these stages, which are charted in advance, the Consultant is evaluated and promoted or terminated.

Due to the considerable pressure and the "up-or-out" policy, turnover among Consultants is high. Attrition averages 15 percent per year at the early stages and increases sharply after the fourth or fifth year. Consultants may move within the industry, outside to one of their clients, or to entrepreneurial endeavors. The most common movement outside the field is to the corporate planning departments of large corporations. It is uncommon for Consultants to move into line positions, however, due to their premium salaries and lack of line experience.

Additional Information

Due to the breadth of expertise on hand and the array of functions for which consulting is available, most firms position themselves to a specific market. Bain, BCG (Boston Consulting Group), and Braxton are positioned as "strategy-only" firms. McKinsey, Booz Allen & Hamilton, and Cresap, McCormick and Paget are noted for the broad array of services that they offer. Hay Associates, Hewitt Associates, and Data Resources are firms that specialize in a particular business function. Finally, the Big Eight accounting firms specialize in MIS (management information services) and small business consulting, although consulting is only one of the services they offer.

Some generalizations can be made about the size of consulting firms. Although there are notable exceptions to this rule, many of the small firms concentrate solely on a particular industry or business function, such as energy, for example, or human resource consulting. These small firms may also limit their activity to a particular geographic region, and they are more likely to assist in the implementation of their ideas. Small specialty firms rarely pay as well as their larger counterparts and are less likely to hire new MBAs without prior work experience in their specialty.

As is often true in other industries, it is easier to move from a large consulting firm to a small one than vice versa. Small firms often give new Consultants greater responsibility and exposure to clients, and the technical skills learned in the small firm can be highly marketable.

The following sections include information on specific areas of consulting. Unless otherwise specified, the function, routine, skills, compensation, and career paths of these consultants mirror those previously discussed.

Sources of Additional Information

See Diane McKinney-Kellogg, "Contrasting Successful and Unsuccessful OD Consultation Relationships," in *Group and Organization Studies*, June 1984.

CONSULTING: PUBLIC SECTOR

Education (degrees)	BA	MBA	PhD
Experience required (yrs)	None	1-3	3+
Location	Urban	Rural	Regional / Travel
Compensation ($/yr)	< $25K	$25-30K	$30-35K / >$35K
Work involvement (hrs/wk)	< 50	50-60	> 60
Pace	Relaxed	Medium	Frenetic
Career path (a la Driver)	Spiral	Steady	Linear
Interpersonal style	Loner	Moderate	Outgoing
Cognitive style	Sequential Rules Details	Mixed Principles Systems	Random Free form Big picture
Variety (preference for)	No change Ordered	Occasional Change	Ambiguous Changing

Job Description/Typical Day

Consulting firms that service the public sector specialize in such areas as program planning and evaluation, regulatory economics, technical R&D, economic and industrial development, urban and regional planning, and information systems. Consultants in these firms are more specialized and technically trained than their counterparts in general consulting firms. In addition to the skills required of all consultants, the Government Consultant needs an understanding of bureaucratic problems (i.e., the interrelationships of political, administration, and policy considerations) and compatibility with the government/bureaucratic environment. Government Consultants must deal with extensive documentation and proposal preparation, for massive amounts of detail and technical data must often be mobilized.

The Government Consultant's life-style is far less intense than that of a Strategy Consultant, and an 8-to-5 schedule five days a week is customary. Compensation is estimated to be approximately 20 percent less than that of Strategy Consultants.

Typical Career Paths

Because the organizational structure of these types of firms is fairly flat, there is little opportunity for upward mobility. Once the consultant is known for his or her specialty, he or she will have easy access to high-level government positions or to corporations utilizing that expertise.

Some Employers

Booz Allen & Hamilton (New York, New York): Institutional and Public Management Division, in Washington, D.C.

Cambridge Research (Cambridge, Massachusetts)

Cresap, McCormick and Paget, Inc. (New York, New York): 25 percent of revenues from governmental work, in Washington, D.C.

A. T. Kearney (Chicago, Illinois)

Arthur D. Little (Cambridge, Massachusetts) Policy analysis, environmental-impact statements.

McKinsey & Co. (New York, New York)

McManis Associates (Washington, D.C.)

Resource Planning Associates (Cambridge, Massachusetts): 50 percent of revenues from government work; energy and environmental issues.

SRI (Stanford Research Institute) (Menlo Park, California): 65 percent of revenues from federal government; heavily involved in R&D and policy analysis.

Temple, Barker and Sloane (Lexington, Massachusetts): Policy formulation and program evaluation in terms of business/government interface.

CONSULTING: HUMAN RESOURCES

	BA	MBA	PhD
Education (degrees)	BA	MBA	PhD
Experience required (yrs)	None	1-3	3+
Location	Urban	Rural	Regional / Travel
Compensation ($/yr)	< $25K	$25-30K	$30-35K / >$35K
Work involvement (hrs/wk)	< 50	50-60	> 60
Pace	Relaxed	Medium	Frenetic
Career path (a la Driver)	Spiral	Steady	Linear
Interpersonal style	Loner	Moderate	Outgoing
Cognitive style	Sequential Rules Details	Mixed Principles Systems	Random Free form Big picture
Variety (preference for)	No change Ordered	Occasional Change	Ambiguous Changing

INTRODUCTION

The importance of the human resource management function is growing, due to the acceleration of such trends as government-mandated employment policies, and concern with productivity and the quality of work life. Competition from the Japanese, in particular, provides real impetus for American managers to maximize available human resources.

The field promises new challenge for the 1980s in the following areas: labor-employee relations, union avoidance, and retraining and career development. Demand for MBA skills is up significantly, and the field is becoming more complex—particularly in the areas of executive compensation and manpower planning and forecasting. (See Personnel/Human Resources, Section 9.)

Job Description/Typical Day

The Human Resource Consultant provides assistance in many areas, including organizational planning and career development; outplacement programs; job enrichment; manpower planning and forecasting; executive compensation and benefit programs; and the administration of OSHA, EEO, and Affirmative Action.

Skills

In addition to the general skills needed in consulting, a Human Resource Consultant must have ability and interest in mediation and negotiation, ability to understand and communicate in the corporate culture, an understanding of compensation and employee benefit programs, and an understanding of the regulations currently affecting human resource management.

Compensation

Human Resource Consultants generally earn more than their corporate personnel office counterparts but less than strategic consultants (no figures).

Typical Career Paths

Since compensation is higher than in corporate positions, a Human Resource Consultant may feel constrained by "silver manacles." In the consulting firm, the consultant is in the mainstream of the business, while in a corporate setting, human resources is often a low-status staff job.

There are a number of alternatives to a career in a large consulting firm:

Corporate personnel. Given the foregoing considerations, charting a path at entry is an important consideration due to the wide variations in importance of the function at different companies.

Small consulting practice or own practice. Due to the low entry barriers, there are numerous three- to five-person firms in a given specialty. Currently, outplacement services and compensation management firms are very active.

Executive search. There are a number of major factors in this field. Generally, individuals who are older and have had extensive exposure to corporate environments are preferred. Search firms whose clients are corporations, not individuals, attempt to fill the needs of top management with outsiders in middle- to upper-level management positions.

Some Employers

In the following list of employers, student researchers have capsulized the primary focus of each company in quotations.

Cresap, Paget and McCormick (New York, New York): General management consulting with human resources an important part of the practice.

Hay Associates (Philadelphia, Pennsylvania): Typically hire four to five MBAs annually. "Management consultants with a human resource emphasis."

Hewitt Associates (Lincolnshire, Illinois, and Stamford, Connecticut): "International firm of consultants specializing in total compensation including planning, design, and administration."

Towers, Perrin, Forster, and Crosby (New York, New York, and Boston, Massachusetts): "Human resource management consultants."

Sources of Additional Information

"Career Development Activities—Staffing Human Resource Functions: The Role of the MBA," *The Career Development Bulletin,* Vol. 2, no. 3, 1981.

"The Expanding Role of the Personnel Function," Cambridge, Mass: *Harvard Business Review,* March–April 1975.

"Human Resources, Functions in Transition," Chicago: Heidrick & Struggles, Inc. (International Executive Recruiters), 1977.

"MBA—Management/Business Advice," *Working Woman,* November 1981.

"Personnel: A New Route to the Top," *International Management,* May 1977.

"Personnel Salaries: A Survey, Part I," *Personnel Journal,* December 1981.

"Profile of a Chief Personnel Executive," Chicago: Heidrick & Struggles, Inc., 1977.

Some Consulting Firms and Human Resource Activities

	Management development	Executive compensation	Benefits	Executive recruiting	Career development
Barron-Clayton, Inc.	X			X	
David T. Barry Associates	X			X	X
Booz Allen & Hamilton	X	X		X	X
Cresap, McCormick and Paget	X	X	X		X
Harbridge House	X				X
Hay Associates		X		X	
Hewitt Associates		X	X		
Management Analysis Center	X	X	X		X
McKinsey & Company, Inc.	X	X	X		X
Meredith Associates	X	X	X		X
Olney Associates	X	X	X		
Rath & Strong			X	X	X

CONSULTING: MANAGEMENT INFORMATION SERVICES

	BA	MBA	PhD
Education (degrees)	BA	MBA	PhD
Experience required (yrs)	None	1-3	3+
Location	Urban	Rural	Regional / Travel
Compensation ($/yr)	< $25K	$25-30K	$30-35K / >$35K
Work involvement (hrs/wk)	< 50	50-60	> 60
Pace	Relaxed	Medium	Frenetic
Career path (a la Driver)	Spiral	Steady	Linear
Interpersonal style	Loner	Moderate	Outgoing
Cognitive style	Sequential Rules Details	Mixed Principles Systems	Random Free form Big picture
Variety (preference for)	No change Ordered	Occasional Change	Ambiguous Changing

INTRODUCTION

MIS consulting services are most often provided by small software companies or the larger general-purpose consent companies in the Big Eight CPA firms. In the small software companies, a technical background is required. In the larger firms, computer experience is beneficial but not necessary. Once an MBA enters this area as a Staff Analyst, however, he or she will have to be constantly training to learn and stay up with the computer field. The MIS consultant's main task will be to design a system or systems to meet the client's information needs.

Compensation

Compensation is comparable to that for general consultants.

Typical Career Path

This area of consulting also faces high attrition due to a prevalent "up-or-out" policy, yet constant exposure to private industry and sound technological background give MIS consultants alternative career paths. At the Staff Analyst (entry) level, there are opportunities to go into hardware or software marketing organizations. At the Manager level, opportunities exist for private industry's data processing divisions or transfer to other consulting firms or to hard/software marketing organizations.

Some Employers

For MBAs, the Big Eight and big multipurpose consulting firms are best. The Big Eight tend to pay less but train better. (See Public Accounting, Section 36.)

CONSULTING: NONPROFIT

Education (degrees)	BA	MBA	PhD
Experience required (yrs)	None	1-3	3+
Location	Urban	Rural	Regional / Travel
Compensation ($/yr)	< $25K	$25-30K	$30-35K / >$35K
Work involvement (hrs/wk)	< 50	50-60	> 60
Pace	Relaxed	Medium	Frenetic
Career path (a la Driver)	Spiral	Steady	Linear
Interpersonal style	Loner	Moderate	Outgoing
Cognitive style	Sequential / Rules / Details	Mixed / Principles / Systems	Random / Free form / Big picture
Variety (preference for)	No change / Ordered	Occasional / Change	Ambiguous / Changing

Job Description/Typical Day

Nonprofit Consultants provide an array of services for museums, hospitals, libraries, labor and credit unions, foundations, and issue-related social change groups. Nonprofit consulting is more "process oriented" than are other ("result-oriented") forms of consulting. Nonprofit clients are often quite conservative and hesitate to make changes without being led through the analysis and shown, as much as possible, a guarantee of the results. For Nonprofit Consultants, therefore, interpersonal and communicative skills are more important than quantitative analytical skills.

The life-style of a Nonprofit Consultant is one of constant intermingling of personal and professional time, yet the work pace is more relaxed, informal, and low key.

Nonprofit consulting firms can be divided into new and old school or those who treat nonprofit institutions in a nonprofit context and those who do not. The new school uses more financial analysis and quantitative methods than does the old. Both schools, however, must be sensitive to the purposes and concerns of the organization.

Typical Career Paths

The organizational structure of many nonprofit consulting firms is largely horizontal, so that vertical career advancement is minimal. The transition from nonprofit to profit consulting is difficult; the reverse is easier.

Some Employers

ABT Associates, Inc. (Cambridge, Massachusetts)
Booz Allen & Hamilton (New York, New York)
Cambridge Associates (Cambridge, Massachusetts)
Arthur D. Little (Cambridge, Massachusetts)
McKinsey & Company (New York, New York)
Volunteer Urban Consulting Group (New York, New York)

Health Care Consultants

Academy of Health Care Consultants (Chicago, Illinois)
American Academy of Health Administration (Texarkana, Texas)

CONSULTING: STRATEGIC

Education (degrees)	BA	MBA	PhD
Experience required (yrs)	None	1-3	3+
Location	Urban	Rural	Regional / Travel
Compensation ($/yr)	< $25K	$25-30K	$30-35K / >$35K
Work involvement (hrs/wk)	< 50	50-60	> 60
Pace	Relaxed	Medium	Frenetic
Career path (a la Driver)	Spiral	Steady	Linear
Interpersonal style	Loner	Moderate	Outgoing
Cognitive style	Sequential Rules Details	Mixed Principles Systems	Random Free form Big picture
Variety (preference for)	No change Ordered	Occasional Change	Ambiguous Changing

Job Description/Typical Day

Strategy consulting is currently considered the elite or "highbrow" sector of consulting. Strategy Consultants examine the skills, resources, and nature of their client's business and chart an appropriate course for their future. Strategy Consultants serve as additional staff for their clients in the corporate planning area. Movement into the planning department of large corporations is, therefore, easy.

The daily work environment also varies between firms. Bain strongly favors team interaction, with required meetings every two to three days. BCG expects consultants to work more as individuals, with occasional team meetings. McKinsey consultants average two days of travel per week, while the BCG staff averages two days every three weeks.

Skills

Conceptual, analytical, and interpersonal skills are most highly valued for Strategy Consultants. Different firms stress different skills, however. BCG and Bain are interested in academic excellence and hire from the best MBA schools while McKinsey and Booz Allen & Hamilton place an emphasis on prior work experience and hire a substantial number of employees directly from business occupations.

Compensation

BCG and Bain start MBAs at $40,000 to $45,000 or more; Booz Allen & Hamilton and McKinsey start at $35,000 to $40,000; and the Big Eight accounting firms that handle strategic consulting start as low as $20,000.

Some Employers

Some of the most notable strategy consulting firms are:

Arthur D. Little (Cambridge, Massachusetts)
Bain and Company (Boston, Massachusetts)
Booz Allen & Hamilton (New York, New York)
Boston Consulting Group (Boston, Massachusetts)
Braxton Associates (Boston, Massachusetts)
Cresap, McCormick & Paget (New York, New York)
McKinsey & Company (New York, New York)
Resources Planning Associates (Cambridge, Massachusetts)
Temple, Barker and Sloane (Lexington, Massachusetts)

CONSULTING: TECHNICAL

	BA	MBA	PhD
Education (degrees)	BA	MBA	PhD
Experience required (yrs)	None	1-3	3+
Location	Urban	Rural	Regional / Travel
Compensation ($/yr)	< $25K	$25-30K	$30-35K / >$35K
Work involvement (hrs/wk)	< 50	50-60	> 60
Pace	Relaxed	Medium	Frenetic
Career path (a la Driver)	Spiral	Steady	Linear
Interpersonal style	Loner	Moderate	Outgoing
Cognitive style	Sequential Rules Details	Mixed Principles Systems	Random Free form Big picture
Variety (preference for)	No change Ordered	Occasional Change	Ambiguous Changing

Job Description/Typical Day

Although the large, generalist consulting firms cover most technical specialties, the strongest growth in this area is from small one-industry/specialty firms. These firms are less likely to hire new MBAs without significant technical backgrounds. In small firms, particularly, the entry-level consultant may be expected to study at night for an engineering or other technical certification.

Skills

The technical skills required of these consultants are highly marketable, so movement between consulting firms and into private industry is fairly free.

Compensation

Entry-level salaries typically range from the high-20s to the mid-30s.

Some Employers

General Consulting Firms

Arthur D. Little (Cambridge, Massachusetts)
Booz Allen & Hamilton (New York, New York)
ICF, Inc. (Washington, D.C.)
Temple, Barker and Sloane (Lexington, Massachusetts)

Energy Specialists

Energy and Environmental Assoc. (Arlington, Virginia)
Energy Resources Company (Dallas, Texas)
Resources Planning Associates (Cambridge, Massachusetts)

Technology and Other Specialists

Combustion Engineering (Stamford, Connecticut)
Data Resources, Inc. (Lexington, Massachusetts)
Mitre/Mitre (Washington, D.C.)
National Economic Research Association (Washington, D.C.)
Charles River Associates (Cambridge, MA)
Science Applications, Inc. (La Jolla, California)
SRI (Stanford Research Institute) (Menlo Park, California)
TRW Energy Systems, Inc. (Solon, Ohio)

MIS

The Big Eight accounting firms (see Public Accounting, Section 36)

23   ENTERTAINMENT

INTRODUCTION

The MBA does not provide automatic entry into the entertainment industry as it does in other fields. The "creative" people who have traditionally run this business have resisted the "bottom-line" orientation of the MBA. This resistance has waned in recent years, however, as rising production costs, international distribution, and the growth of television movies and cable television have required more sophisticated forms of financing and marketing. Still, the door is barely open to the MBA without related experience. A primary prerequisite for successfully entering this industry is a firm commitment to it, followed by excellent interpersonal skills, aggressiveness, perseverance, contacts, and luck.

Entry-level positions vary substantially and are often humble ones, for most executives in the industry today began at the bottom (e.g., as pages or clerks). There are virtually no set career paths and very few training programs.

The industry is a glamorous one, however, and the potential for financial rewards is extremely high.

ENTERTAINMENT: FILM INDUSTRY

Education (degrees)	BA	MBA	PhD
Experience required (yrs)	None	1-3	3+
Location	Urban	Rural	Regional / Travel
Compensation ($/yr)	$< $25K	$25-30K	$30-35K / $>$35K
Work involvement (hrs/wk)	$<$ 50	50-60	$>$ 60
Pace	Relaxed	Medium	Frenetic
Career path (a la Driver)	Spiral	Steady	Linear
Interpersonal style	Loner	Moderate	Outgoing
Cognitive style	Sequential Rules Details	Mixed Principles Systems	Random Free form Big picture
Variety (preference for)	No change Ordered	Occasional Change	Ambiguous Changing

Job Description/Typical Day

Most large film companies hire MBAs for either Financial or Marketing Analyst positions. The activities performed in these positions are similar to those performed in any other industry. These positions can lead, however, to opportunities in distribution, financing, or production. Most executives of the large film companies have production experience.

In a large film studio, production is divided between the Executive Producer and Creative Producer. The Executive Producer handles the financial and business arrangements of a film project and usually comes up through the ranks of the studio. The Executive Producer is employed on a salaried basis and requires MBA-related skills. The Creative Producer serves as the liaison between the creative and financial people and handles the administrative and production details.

Due to the rapid growth of television movies and cable television, most films are now being made by small independent producers who sell them to the large studios for distribution. The Independent Producer, who combines the function of Executive and Creative Producer, arranges a film's financing either through a studio or an investment bank that creates a limited partnership as a tax shelter. Given contacts and perseverance, an MBA can often enter this area as an Assistant Producer.

Skills

The primary requisite is a love of the industry, followed by persistence, aggressiveness, and an ability to deal with highly ambiguous situations.

Compensation

Compensation varies considerably at the entry level depending upon the position. The most likely range is $20,000 to $30,000. After that the income potential can reach into the millions depending upon the career path taken.

Typical Career Path

Reputation and past performance are essential in the film industry, so there is little cross-functional transfer for producers, directors, and so on. The most likely career progression for producers is to the top executive positions in the large studios; however, this often means less income and freedom.

Some Employers

Columbia (New York, New York)
Disney (Anaheim, California)
Filmways (Los Angeles, California)
MGM (Culver City, California)
Paramount (New York, New York)

20th Century-Fox (Beverly Hills, California)
United Artists (New York, New York)
Universal (Los Angeles, California)
Warner Communications (Burbank, California)

Sources of Additional Information

Billboard
Performing Arts
Variety

Industry personnel

ENTERTAINMENT: PERFORMING ARTS MANAGEMENT

Education (degrees)	BA	MBA	PhD
Experience required (yrs)	None	1-3	3+
Location	Urban	Rural	Regional / Travel
Compensation ($/yr)	< $25K	$25-30K	$30-35K / >$35K
Work involvement (hrs/wk)	< 50	50-60	> 60
Pace	Relaxed	Medium	Frenetic
Career path (a la Driver)	Spiral	Steady	Linear
Interpersonal style	Loner	Moderate	Outgoing
Cognitive style	Sequential Rules Details	Mixed Principles Systems	Random Free form Big picture
Variety (preference for)	No change Ordered	Occasional Change	Ambiguous Changing

Job Description/Typical Day

The duties of a Performing Arts Manager include management of artists and art facilities, advertising, promotion, contract negotiation, and tour arrangements. Few MBAs hold these positions, yet the financial and marketing skills learned in business school are a great asset to a Performing Arts Manager.

Skills

The primary skills and requirements for the position are a knowledge of the arts, understanding of contracts, and an ability to negotiate. Since people are your products, interpersonal skills are essential. Performing Arts Managers are independent, creative, and enthusiastic and must be able to work well with large groups of people and in unstructured environments.

This job requires long hours, extensive travel, and continuous decision making. The progression along the career path is often mirrored by a geographical progression from small metropolitan areas to larger ones. Sixty percent of all Performing Arts Managers work in New York.

Compensation

Compensation at the entry level is low compared with average MBA salaries. One reason for this is that entry-level positions are often with small regional companies or nonprofit organizations. There is potential for rapid advancement into large metropolitan associations, however, with commensurate salary increases.

Typical Career Paths

A typical MBA career path might begin as the Business Manager of a small national company (such as the National Theater of the Deaf), followed by Assistant Manager of a large metropolitan organization (such as the Boston Symphony Orchestra). Two to five years of experience in this position could then lead to a position as manager of a large organization (such as the San Francisco Opera Company) for five to ten years.

Future career opportunities might include a Personal Manager of top artists, Facilities Manager (e.g., Madison Square Garden), Public Sector Manager (e.g., National Endowment for the Arts), or movie/record company Manager.

Some Employers

Arts facilities (Schubert Theatres)
Big-name individual artists (Leonard Bernstein)
Dance companies (Joffrey Ballet)
Major symphonies (Boston Symphony)
Museums (Detroit Historical Museum)

National Endowment for the Arts
Small national performing companies (Martha Graham Dance Company)
Theater companies (American Repertory)

Sources of Additional Information

Magazines (*Variety, Billboard, Performing Arts,* etc.)
Industry personnel
Conferences
Books

24   ENTREPRENEURING

INTRODUCTION

In some ways, careers in entrepreneuring are incompatible with business schools and their graduates. Some critics believe that because of the structure and routine of the educational process, earning a degree in business squeezes out of people the very things they need to be successful entrepreneurs, such as creativity, unconventional thinking, a broad perspective, and a willingness to accept risk. Perhaps, perhaps not. Still, the personal characteristics that support entrepreneurial activity are not all developed in business schools. Given that the vast majority of corporations established each year fail, entrepreneurs need to have reservoirs of resiliency in addition to their desires to do things better, their willingness to take calculated risks, their willingness to work long hours, their abilities to marshal resources, and their drive to build something.

Some schools are acting on this concern either by offering courses in entrepreneurial skills, or by encouraging non-conformist behavior, something most entrepreneurs seem to exhibit. At Stanford, Michael Ray has been offering a course on creative thinking designed, in part, to stimulate fresh ways of approaching business problems, a skill that would benefit entrepreneurs.

We have divided entrepreneuring into two parts: Small Business Management and Starting New Ventures. The former requires a willingness to live within a framework established by someone else, while bringing to that framework business skill and a desire to make the business grow. The latter requires prodigious amounts of energy and analytic and interpersonal skill to beat the odds of failure. The former presents probable road blocks to the top position, the latter poses high degrees of risk

Many who start new businesses get caught up in what has become known as "Founder's Syndrome," the belief held by some founders that they can manage something that has grown beyond the start-up stage when really their skills are limited to start-up activities. There are few who seem able to make the transition from start-up management to the more routinized, long-term professional management needed to control and grow a much larger organization. Founders who understand their skills and limitations are better able to pass the reins of leadership on to others; those who do not, can stifle and even endanger the growth of the firm. There have been some who have made this transition, David Packard and Bill Hewlett for two, but many more have failed. If you are thinking about starting your own venture, we encourage you to be realistic about your skills. If you are thinking about going to work for a founder, we encourage you to assess his or her skills carefully and sort out the probabilities of making a successful transition well in advance.

ENTREPRENEURING: SMALL BUSINESS MANAGEMENT

Education (degrees)	BA	MBA	PhD
Experience required (yrs)	None	1-3	3+
Location	Urban	Rural	Regional / Travel
Compensation ($/yr)	< $25K	$25-30K	$30-35K / >$35K
Work involvement (hrs/wk)	< 50	50-60	> 60
Pace	Relaxed	Medium	Frenetic
Career path (a la Driver)	Spiral	Steady	Linear
Interpersonal style	Loner	Moderate	Outgoing
Cognitive style	Sequential Rules Details	Mixed Principles Systems	Random Free form Big picture
Variety (preference for)	No change Ordered	Occasional Change	Ambiguous Changing

Job Description/Typical Day

Small business management covers a wide spectrum of opportunities, and job descriptions, therefore, tend to be general and multifaceted. Small businesses offer positions in a wide variety of functions and industries, including some unique situations.

In very small companies, a new MBA might function as a General Manager, but more typically enters in a specific function. A newly hired MBA usually receives immediate responsibility and is expected to justify his or her salary with performance from the start. Through such exposure the Small Business Manager can expect to develop rapidly.

Most sources indicate that a Small Business Manager often works long hours (55 to 70 per week) but is afforded some degree of flexibility in managing the time. His or her results are weighed more heavily than are appearances, efforts, or potential.

Skills

The skills required of Small Business Managers are as varied as their duties. These individuals must be versatile, practical, flexible, persistent and creative self-starters who are results oriented and comfortable in an unstructured environment. They must be able to make decisions quickly and must possess sales and numbers ability. To tie in all these talents and to motivate others, they must have excellent interpersonal skills.

Compensation

Compensation for MBAs joining small business, according to the placement office at UVA's Darden School, are the most negotiated and customized of any area of MBA employment. Starting salaries tend to be 20 to 25 percent below the average for the graduating class as a whole. These low salaries are often counterbalanced, however, by a future equity interest in the firm, usually in the form of stock options. (Get it in writing whenever possible.) If you go to work for the owner-manager, he or she will expect you to prove yourself so valuable that you will have to be given a piece of the action to keep you. Until then, the owner will expect you to be worth more than he or she is paying you—an owner won't just give equity away.

Typical Career Paths

Career paths vary with the size, complexity, and culture of the small company. Some MBAs are hired directly into the General Manager slot, linking their future with their ability to obtain equity and make the company prosper. More frequently, an MBA is hired into a relatively high-level functional position and can aspire to obtain equity and eventually take over as general manager.

The experience gained from working for a small business is excellent general business training—perhaps even the best you can get, short of an MBA. Its transferability is, therefore, very high but usually best transferred either into starting your own business later or into another small company.

Some Employers

Finding a job in small business will require a much more creative search process than for most opportunities, largely because most small businesses do not recruit on campus. The search will be a time-consuming process that involves building a network of contacts. Any small firm with sales of $5 million or more is probably a potential employer.

Additional Information

It takes a special kind of person to manage a small business successfully. The risks can be very high, as can be the rewards. Perhaps more so than with a large company, it is important to know yourself, know your spouse, and know the people you will be working with. You and your family will be sacrificing current income and spare time for potential future benefits. These benefits are dependent on the honesty, competence, goals, and hard work of the entire management team. Only you can decide if you fit on that team.

A careful analysis of the company and industry is important. Because there are few people in the organization, the MBA must understand who has what power and what each owner and manager's goals and intentions are. There is no point in working one's fingers to the bone only to have "Junior" step in ahead of you when he graduates from college.

Once you become your own boss, you may find it difficult to go back to a big company if things don't work out. A larger firm often perceives a Small Business Manager as less disciplined and more desirous of autonomy than it would like. The Small Business Manager may likewise resist the loss of a title and the reduction in authority that will often accompany such a move.

Sources of Additional Information

Entrepreneur
Inc.
Money
Venture

See also "The Entrepreneur in You" quiz and article in *Across the Board*, July–August 1984.

ENTREPRENEURING: STARTING NEW VENTURES

	BA	MBA	PhD
Education (degrees)	BA	MBA	PhD
Experience required (yrs)	None	1-3	3+
Location	Urban	Rural	Regional / Travel
Compensation ($/yr)	< $25K	$25-30K	$30-35K / >$35K
Work involvement (hrs/wk)	< 50	50-60	> 60
Pace	Relaxed	Medium	Frenetic
Career path (a la Driver)	Spiral	Steady	Linear
Interpersonal style	Loner	Moderate	Outgoing
Cognitive style	Sequential Rules Details	Mixed Principles Systems	Random Free form Big picture
Variety (preference for)	No change Ordered	Occasional Change	Ambiguous Changing

Job Description/Typical Day

Starting a new venture is an all-encompassing task. The Entrepreneur must act as venture capitalist, marketer, manufacturer, treasurer, personnel officer, office manager, executive, and "grunt." Of course, assistance with these functions may be available, but the Entrepreneur must nevertheless be involved in every aspect of the company.

Extreme amounts of time and energy are consumed in a start-up. As a consequence, one's life-style is dictated by the needs of the venture. Family, recreation, and personal interest often take a back seat, creating pressures on the individual and those around him or her. Time pressures, financial pressures, and personal pressures often occur simultaneously. Because of the personal sacrifices dictated by beginning a new venture, the entrepreneur must have the full commitment of his or her spouse.

Skills

Much information suggests that there is no one personality type for a successful Entrepreneur. Some are highly successful in large corporate settings before beginning on their own, while others are business failures. One particular characteristic that all successful Entrepreneurs have is perseverance. In addition, they have a very high need for achievement. These are people who strive to make things happen. Another characteristic is the ability to sell—to sell themselves, their ideas, their plans, and, eventually, their product. The Entrepreneur must be a self-starter and be able to create his or her own structure. Finally, the entrepreneur must be a risk taker.

There is one factor that disqualifies a person from being an Entrepreneur; the need for status. If you feel the need to be associated with the upper classes, this is not the occupation for you.

Compensation

This is one of the most alluring aspects of starting a new venture. The income potential is almost unlimited. Initial income may be nonexistent, however, and should be considered when capitalizing the firm.

Typical Career Paths

Once the enterprise is running and successful, there are two choices for the Entrepreneur, depending on his or her needs and style: the undertaking can be operated as a business or it can be sold for someone else to run. Upon sale or merger, the former owner will likely be asked to provide some assistance for a period.

The Entrepreneur, whether successful or not, is not a good candidate for employment in a large and structured business. The independent approach gained while on one's own seldom sits well with large companies. It is, therefore, much easier to go from a large company to a new venture than the reverse.

Employers

You!

Additional Information

Between 80 and 90 percent of new ventures fail. Management incompetence is the cause 90 percent of the time, which includes both business ignorance and business irresponsibility.

The three areas of risk that the individual needs to consider are financial, career, and psychic. Often the Entrepreneur must be prepared to risk all of his or her assets. Typically, little or no salary is taken during the start-up phase. The big payoff comes in the form of capital gains, if the venture is successful. Failure in a new venture can seriously hinder career plans, hurting the Entrepreneur's reputation and also making it difficult to get a job, even in an unrelated area. The rewards come in the form of valuable experience in all phases of a business, and success gives flexibility to coordinate personal, career, and life-style goals. The deep and pervasive involvement of the individual in the venture can envelop the whole life-style of a person. Failure can be devastating, depending on the personality. Some individuals never recover their self-confidence. The rewards of success are similarly pervasive. The sense of autonomy, responsibility, and accomplishment from a good start-up can be the biggest payoff to the entrepreneur.

Once the potential Entrepreneur decides that starting his or her own firm is the type of activity that best fits his or her future goals, the following questions need to be asked: Is there a market need? What do I offer the customer? What are the keys to success in this market? Do I control the keys? How much money do I need? Where do I get it?

In the following section, we have considered in greater detail the thought process that is necessary in developing a new business, in this case an import-export company.

Issues To Consider In Entering International Business

1. *What are you going to import?*

   What are the domestic market characteristics of your product(s)? (Market and industry situation analysis, competitive analysis, etc.)

   Is test marketing your product(s) required?

   Do you need to establish a customer base before importing?

2. *What are the sourcing considerations?*

   Locate all possible sources of supply (use embassies, consulates, Chambers of Commerce, personal contacts, and visits to find supplier).

   Can you find manufacturers (suppliers) of this product in more than one country? If so, which source(s) provide(s) the highest profit possibilities and the lowest risk (consider the *final* cost after entering the domestic country, not just the initial price of goods)?

Research government regulations regarding your product(s) in both the exporting and importing countries involved: tariffs, countervailing taxes, required licenses.

Is a business/government/industry/economy-style country analysis necessary for your product (i.e., cars, equipment, components)? If so, consider especially the political environment, foreign currency status, balance of payments, and so on.

Are you going to import a product(s) once or on a continuous basis? If continuous, establishing a solid buying relationship with your manufacturer is important. Know whom you are dealing with, who has the authority to make changes in decisions like delivery dates, who is the financial officer—know as much as is possible about the financial status and history of the manufacturer, as well as who its customers are and who are potential competitors in your country.

3. *How are you going to act?*

Will you act as a manufacturer's representative, agent (getting a supplier and a buyer together), independent importer, or only wholesaler? (If you are acting as a wholesaler and not a *direct* importer, consider the preceding sourcing questions in terms of the importing/warehousing companies you may be using.)

Will you require customs brokers or will you handle brokering yourself?

Do you need an import license?

4. *What agreement do you want to negotiate with your supplier?*

Exclusivity.

Prices, quantities, product specifications, delivery dates.

Returned (damaged) goods liability policy.

Insurance.

Shipping.

Terms and means of payment (learn how to handle letters of credit and the international banking system—your bank will apprise you of policies, options; establish a good relationship with the banker handling your account).

5. *What is your specific business objective?*

Growth, financial limitations, regionality, desired market position. Where do you want to be in the long term? What plans must be made now for later expansion and diversification?

Most fledgling importing companies report that initial success depends on how creative you are in marketing your product, how competitive you are price-wise (which reflects the quality of your sourcing agreement), how dependable your product quality and delivery systems are, how financially flexible you are, how much energy you are willing to commit to your business, how much risk you are willing to take, and how strong is your network of manufacturers, bankers, and customers. Your compensation depends entirely on what percentage of profit you must reinvest and what you can retain.

Sources of Additional Information

See previous chapter.

See also Gordon B. Baty, *Entrepreneurship: Playing to Win,* Reston Va: Reston, 1974; and "Who Are the Harvard Self-Employed," *Harvard Business School Bulletin*, April 1984.

25 FAST FOODS

	BA	MBA	PhD
Education (degrees)	BA	MBA	PhD
Experience required (yrs)	None	1-3	3+
Location	Urban	Rural	Regional / Travel
Compensation ($/yr)	< $25K	$25-30K	$30-35K / >$35K
Work involvement (hrs/wk)	< 50	50-60	> 60
Pace	Relaxed	Medium	Frenetic
Career path (a la Driver)	Spiral	Steady	Linear
Interpersonal style	Loner	Moderate	Outgoing
Cognitive style	Sequential Rules Details	Mixed Principles Systems	Random Free form Big picture
Variety (preference for)	No change Ordered	Occasional Change	Ambiguous Changing

Job Description/Typical Day

Few MBAs go into restaurant management. Entry-level positions are usually line management jobs in single fast-food units.

The job requires long hours, attention to detail, an ability to supervise 10 to 20 employees (along with an ability to deal with high turnover), a commitment to corporate philosophy, and a concern for people.

Compensation

The manager of a fast-food unit can expect to make between $15,000 and $25,000 plus a bonus based on sales.

Career Path

The career path would be Assistant Manager of a Unit to Manager to Manager of Multiple Units and finally to corporate headquarters in a variety of positions.

Some Employers

McDonalds Corp. (Hinsdale, Illinois)
Burger King (division of Pillsbury) (Miami, Florida)
Pizza Hut (division of Pepsi) (Wichita, Kansas)
Howard Johnson Company (Braintree, Massachusetts)
Wendys International (Dublin, Ohio)

None are likely to solicit MBAs. In general, job opportunities will be the result of an MBA's initiative.

Education (degrees)	BA	MBA	PhD
Experience required (yrs)	None	1-3	3+
Location	Urban	Rural	Regional / Travel
Compensation ($/yr)	< $25K	$25-30K	$30-35K / >$35K
Work involvement (hrs/wk)	< 50	50-60	> 60
Pace	Relaxed	Medium	Frenetic
Career path (a la Driver)	Spiral	Steady	Linear
Interpersonal style	Loner	Moderate	Outgoing
Cognitive style	Sequential Rules Details	Mixed Principles Systems	Random Free form Big picture
Variety (preference for)	No change Ordered	Occasional Change	Ambiguous Changing

Job Description/Typical Day

The MBA in federal government is usually hired into one of the following positions: Policy Analyst, Budget Analyst, Program Analyst, Financial Analyst, Grants Specialist, or Staff Aide.

Ninety percent of federal government jobs are located in Washington, D.C., and bring little chance of transfer. This benefits the dual-career family interested in settling in a large urban area. The work load varies depending upon your branch of government, direct supervisor, and proximity to cabinet-level decisions. Travel is light; rarely over 15 percent. Some international travel can be expected in the departments of Treasury, State, Commerce, Agriculture, and Defense and in the National Security Council.

Those entering the civil service system have exceptional job security. Those with "career status" also have the ability to reenter the system noncompetitively and are given preference in transfers both within and between agencies.

There are psychological benefits and drawbacks. The benefits include service to one's country, exciting and varied work, and the feeling of closeness to the seat of political power. The drawbacks include the low status of most government jobs and the limitations imposed by the relatively low pay scale.

Skills

Writing and interpersonal skills are of the foremost importance. Due to the predominance of communication via memo, writing skills are more critical in government than in business. Interpersonal skills are also necessary to facilitate dealing within and between government agencies. Government employees are rarely fired so you must be able to get along with your peers. Most entry-level jobs are analyst positions that, therefore, require proficiency with numbers and a knowledge of finance and/or control. Other, less tangible, skills include the ability to "survive in a hectic environment," having an "acceptable" personality, not rocking the boat, and accepting not being judged on the bottom line.

Compensation

The 1981 Harvard MBAs' goverment compensation ranged from $25,000 to $38,800, with the median salary $34,500. Those entering the government without prior experience begin between levels GS8 and GS11. Benefits such as pension and insurance programs are excellent, and vacation benefits range from two to four weeks.

Typical Career Paths

MBAs usually enter the government at two different periods in their careers: as a first job or as a political appointee at the top levels. At the entry level, the salaries are somewhat lower than average for graduating MBAs, but at two or three years this evens out. By six years into a career, however, the difference between public and private sector salaries is so great that a transfer to the public sector causes hardship. Transfer in midcareer is further complicated by the government's preference for hiring from within. MBAs with both public and private sector experience recommend private sector jobs for one or two years before government. This builds the necessary credibility with the private sector that you will need if you want to shuttle between the two.

Transferability back to the private sector may be affected by recent legislation on conflict of interest. While this applies most clearly to top-level officials, inquiries should be made before taking a position.

27 GENETIC ENGINEERING

Education (degrees)	BA	MBA	PhD
Experience required (yrs)	None	1-3	3+
Location	Urban	Rural	Regional / Travel
Compensation ($/yr)	< $25K	$25-30K	$30-35K / >$35K
Work involvement (hrs/wk)	< 50	50-60	> 60
Pace	Relaxed	Medium	Frenetic
Career path (a la Driver)	Spiral	Steady	Linear
Interpersonal style	Loner	Moderate	Outgoing
Cognitive style	Sequential Rules Details	Mixed Principles Systems	Random Free form Big picture
Variety (preference for)	No change Ordered	Occasional Change	Ambiguous Changing

Job Description/Typical Day

Genetic engineering is an emerging industry populated by large, established companies and small, entrepreneurial firms. Regardless of the size of the enterprise, research and development is the critical function. Market research, market development, and strategic planning are the key business and managerial functions, as it is necessary to identify the most fruitful future commercial opportunities. Marketing and planning information must be obtained from informal contacts with people in the field, as there are few formal conferences, trade organizations, or published sources at this time.

Skills

General management skills are becoming increasingly important as companies move from R&D projects to the production and marketing of viable consumer products. Although this field will eventually incorporate all business functions, current requirements make a technical background a decided advantage. This type of high-technology industry is characterized by an unstructured environment and requires creative thinking.

Compensation

No base of information is available. There is potential for equity positions in small firms. Some of the major players in the field are large pharmaceutical, chemical, and oil companies offering salaries competitive with other MBA opportunities.

Typical Career Paths

Large firms have entered this field through in-house research, joint ventures with new firms, and equity interests in these same firms. Since these and other large companies will be doing mergers and acquisitions and business development studies in this field, an MBA may be able to enter via involvement in strategic planning for pharmaceutical, chemical, and oil companies. Of course, the possibility exists to link up with scientists to form new ventures, since general managers are essential to the future commercial success of these new businesses.

Another route into genetic engineering is through venture capital. Since the industry has been showing large losses and huge financing needs for a long period, venture capital financing and financial backing from large corporations will be necessary. This can lead to equity interests and business opportunities in the finance area. The eventual need for management personnel familiar with patent laws, government regulations, and other potential legal questions may make this an excellent possibility for a JD/MBA.

Some Employers

Leaders

Bethesda Research Labs (Bethesda, Maryland)
Cetus Corp. (Berkeley, California)
Genentech, Inc. (San Francisco, California)
Genex Corp. (Rockville, Maryland)

Other Companies

DeKalb (DeKalb, Illinois)
Dow (Midland, Michigan)
Du Pont (Wilmington, Delaware)
Fluor (Irvine, California)
Hoffman-LaRoche (Nutley, New Jersey)
Eli Lilly (Indianapolis, Indiana)
Merck (Rahway, New Jersey)
Monsanto (St. Louis, Missouri)
G.D. Searle, Inc. (Skokie, Illinois)
Upjohn (Kalamazoo, Michigan)

In addition, major oil companies are beginning to show significant interest in the field.

Additional Information

Genetic engineering has the potential to become the semiconductor business of the future. Estimates for the overall market by 1990 exceed $15 billion annually. Therefore, the timing is right to enter this field. According to a *Time* article of March 8, 1981,

> The future of such firms (genetic engineering) is complicated further by the fact that few businessmen can really understand the science, and few scientists can comprehend the business mentality.

Sources of Additional Information

Most articles on this industry are in technical publications such as *European Chemical News, Chemical & Engineering News,* and *Chemical Week.*

28 HEALTH CARE INDUSTRY

INTRODUCTION

In recent years the health care field has been America's largest and fastest-growing industry. It has also been traditionally void of MBAs. As health care costs have risen out of control, however, the need and demand for MBAs has increased. We shall examine two opportunities for MBAs in this industry: hospital administration and marketing of health maintenance organizations (HMOs).

HEALTH CARE: HOSPITAL ADMINISTRATION

Education (degrees)	BA	MBA	PhD
Experience required (yrs)	None	1-3	3+
Location	Urban	Rural	Regional / Travel
Compensation ($/yr)	< $25K	$25-30K	$30-35K / >$35K
Work involvement (hrs/wk)	< 50	50-60	> 60
Pace	Relaxed	Medium	Frenetic
Career path (a la Driver)	Spiral	Steady	Linear
Interpersonal style	Loner	Moderate	Outgoing
Cognitive style	Sequential Rules Details	Mixed Principles Systems	Random Free form Big picture
Variety (preference for)	No change Ordered	Occasional Change	Ambiguous Changing

Job Description/Typical Day

Beginning as a Hospital Administration Intern, an MBA learns the business of the health care provider. Most of a Hospital Administrator's time is spent in problem solving or putting out fires. Because of increasing government regulation, the Hospital Administrator spends much time in meetings with government officials at the local and state level. Community liaison activities are also becoming an increasingly important aspect of the manager's position.

Skills

Strong interpersonal skills are needed, for the administrator must deal effectively with all levels of employees, from the chief of staff to the janitor. These dealings require the administrator to be well versed in medicine's technical jargon. The administrator develops yearly operating budgets and capital appropriation plans as well, which require financial and analytical skills.

Within the health care industry, physicians are considered the professionals, and management is often expected to cater to their desires. Consequently, the Administrator must have tact and be able to manage company politics.

Compensation

Starting salaries in internship programs range from $20,000 to the low-30s and higher with prior experience. Salaries vary by region and by hospital; notably, the "name" institutions pay less than their state-run counterparts. As you progress up the hierarchy, salaries are considerably less than in profit-making industries, although the level of responsibility is greater. Employee benefits are substantial, however, and include two to four weeks of vacation, comprehensive insurance and pension programs, payment of professional dues, and often a company car and paid expenses for annual conferences.

Typical Career Paths

Many hospitals have one- to two-year internship programs with staff rotations through functional departments (materials management, nursing, controller's office), and often part of the rotation includes a Staff Assistant position to a department line manager. The end of the rotation leads to a line management position as an Assistant Administrator in a clinical department, such as radiology, surgery, or hematology.

Hospital administration is a rather underdeveloped field for professional managers, and thus the potential for movement is great within and between institutions. It is wise to begin in a "name" teaching hospital as the field is "name" conscious and experience will buy mobility. The top positions at major teaching hospitals are currently held by masters of hospital administration rather than MBAs; however, the MBA can progress from Assistant Administrator to Administrator to Vice-President. Good experience in a major teaching hospital can lead to the Chief Executive Officer position in a 50 to 100 bed hospital within four years.

Some Employers

Cornell University Medical Center (New York, New York)
Duke University Medical Center (Durham, North Carolina)
Johns Hopkins Medical Center (Baltimore, Maryland)
Massachusetts General Hospital (Boston, Massachusetts)
Stanford Medical Center (Palo Alto, California)
University Hospital (New York, New York)
All major teaching hospitals

Profit-Oriented Hospital Holding Companies

American Medical International (Beverly Hills, California)
Hospital Corporation of America (Nashville, Tennessee)
Humana Corporation (Louisville, Kentucky)
National Medical Enterprises (Los Angeles, California)

Sources of Additional Information

American Medical Association (Chicago, Illinois)
All state hospital associations (Massachusetts Hospital Association)
American College of Hospital Administrators (Chicago, Illinois)
Blue Cross/Blue Shield (Richmond, VA)
Health Care Management Review (easy-to-read current reports on finance, management, marketing in the United States)
Health Services Research (scholarly journal of research in all areas of health care delivery)
Hospital Financial Management (simply written monthly on topics of special interest to persons in the management field)
International Journal of Health Services (issue-oriented journal of distinguished international practitioners in the health service fields; high-quality papers on policy, planning, administration, and evaluation)
Medical Group Management Association (Denver, Colorado)
Medical Marketing and Media (monthly news and articles on the marketing of health services and pharmaceuticals)

HEALTH CARE: HEALTH MAINTENANCE ORGANIZATIONS

Education (degrees)	BA	MBA	PhD
Experience required (yrs)	None	1-3	3+
Location	Urban	Rural	Regional / Travel
Compensation ($/yr)	< $25K	$25-30K	$30-35K / >$35K
Work involvement (hrs/wk)	< 50	50-60	> 60
Pace	Relaxed	Medium	Frenetic
Career path (a la Driver)	Spiral	Steady	Linear
Interpersonal style	Loner	Moderate	Outgoing
Cognitive style	Sequential Rules Details	Mixed Principles Systems	Random Free form Big picture
Variety (preference for)	No change Ordered	Occasional Change	Ambiguous Changing

INTRODUCTION

An HMO is an organization of health care personnel and facilities that delivers a comprehensive range of health services to members who enroll voluntarily and pay a fixed, prepaid fee. The prepaid fee covers treatment in HMO facilities and hospitals by a wide range of health care specialists, including physicians, nurses, and allied health professionals.

Doctors receive a salary from the HMO based on standards and qualifications rather than on how many patients they see. Because there is no incentive to deliver unnecessary services, the organization incurs fewer costs and patient premiums can be held down. Studies support the claims that HMO care is more economical. They show that HMO health care bills average 10 to 40 percent less than do other health care alternatives. HMO members tend to go to the hospital only one-third as frequently as do patients under traditional care and lose less time from work.

Corporations have enthusiastically supported the offering of HMO services to their employees because of the cost advantages. This support has led to the rapid development of HMOs throughout the country. MBAs seeking jobs in HMOs have the opportunity to gain entrepreneurial responsibility in a growing industry.

Job Description/Typical Day

The best entry-level position in this field for MBAs is as a Marketing Representative (MR). The Marketing Representative calls on existing and prospective client companies to sell the services of the HMO. He or she deals with the benefits manager of larger firms or the top executives of smaller firms and attempts to educate them on the existence and purpose of HMOs and the advantage to their company's employees of this alternative to traditional health insurance.

Most of the Marketing Representative's day is spent making sales presentations to prospective clients or meeting with employees of existing clients to explain the benefits offered and to enroll them into the plan. The MR entertains a good deal, mostly at lunch, and spends approximately 45 to 50 hours per week on the job. HMOs are located in large and midsized cities, so the representative has the advantages of localized travel and urban settings.

Skills

The most important skills needed for the job are selling and interpersonal skills, flexibility, and organization and drive in an unstructured setting.

Compensation

HMOs hire both MBAs and non-MBAs as Marketing Representatives. They will usually pay only a few thousand dollars premium to MBAs, but will often put them on a fast track. Starting salaries begin at $18,000 to $19,000, but a bonus, based on the number of client companies sold and the number of employees enrolled, can add between $5,000 and $15,000. Employee benefits tend to be strong, with three weeks of vacation and a comprehensive insurance and pension program, as well as an expense account.

Typical Career Paths

An MBA on a fast track would spend one to two years as a Marketing Representative. If the employer owns a chain of HMOs, as do Kaiser or Prudential, he or she would then most likely be transferred to another HMO as a Senior Marketing Representative for a year. A Senior Repesentative does essentially the same job as a Marketing Representative but deals with larger clients and accepts more administrative responsibilities. The next position would be as a Marketing Director for the HMO. The Marketing Director is responsible for the overall marketing operation, including public relations and, with the Director of Administration, reports to the vice president in charge of the HMO. This triumvirate runs the company. After two years or so, the Marketing Director would be promoted and transferred as a Vice-President to run another HMO.

Salaries of top executive positions in HMOs are not high ($45,000 to $55,000 plus bonus), but this job should appeal to someone with an entrepreneurial spirit who wants to run a company with someone else's money.

Some Employers

Blue Cross/Blue Shield Assoc. (Chicago, Illinois)
INA (Philadelphia, Pennsylvania)
Kaiser (Oakland, California)
Prudential (Newark, New Jersey)
Plus many individual HMOs located throughout the country

Sources of Additional Information

See Health Care: Hospital Administration.

29 HOTEL INDUSTRY

Education (degrees)	BA	MBA	PhD
Experience required (yrs)	None	1-3	3+
Location	Urban	Rural	Regional / Travel
Compensation ($/yr)	< $25K	$25-30K	$30-35K / >$35K
Work involvement (hrs/wk)	< 50	50-60	> 60
Pace	Relaxed	Medium	Frenetic
Career path (a la Driver)	Spiral	Steady	Linear
Interpersonal style	Loner	Moderate	Outgoing
Cognitive style	Sequential Rules Details	Mixed Principles Systems	Random Free form Big picture
Variety (preference for)	No change Ordered	Occasional Change	Ambiguous Changing

INTRODUCTION

The hotel industry is less impressed with the MBA degree than with previous hotel experience or hotel and restaurant management school training. Consequently, the MBA is given little or no preferential treatment. Entry-level positions into the industry are varied, but opportunities for MBAs are concentrated in the Financial, Sales/Marketing, or Corporate Planning areas. Management trainees for the operations area are found within the organization or from established university hotel and restaurant management schools.

Hotel employers are looking for those who are committed to the industry and are willing to pay their dues. The time commitment is particularly heavy, for many managers are on call 24 hours a day, seven days a week. Relocation is frequent. Out of 13 top executives surveyed by the *Cornell Hotel and Restaurant Administration Quarterly* (CHRAQ), the majority made three to five moves during their career while 3 moved ten or more times. Compensation is generally low until reaching the top executive level. Two-thirds of the executives were employed by firms with sales of $100 million and reported that they felt underpaid. The two elements of compensation most often cited as needing improvement were base salaries and pension benefits. (Average salaries in 1981 for Assistant Managers were $12,000 to $20,000; for General Managers they were $25,000 to $50,000.)[1]

There are, however, some nice perquisites from working in this industry. Almost all firms provide professional dues, moving expenses, business travel and entertainment expenses, and educational expenses. Many companies also provide cars and free meals.

Job Description/Typical Day

Entry-Level Position in Finance

Internal Auditor—The Auditor focuses on budget controls from a managerial and financial perspective, including the auditing of operational practices.

A typical career path for someone beginning in auditing would be to move next to a hotel property as a Controller, then to the regional office as Assistant Controller, to Controller, and then back to the corporate staff. The eventual top-level position might be as company Treasurer, Comptroller, or Senior Vice-President of Finance.

Entry-Level Positions in Sales/Marketing

Marketing Analyst—An Analyst does basic marketing research and analysis on new and/or existing properties, services, and advertising and promotional programs.

[1]Swanljung, Mikael, "How Hotel Executives Made the Climb to the Top," *The Cornell Hotel and Restaurant Administration Quarterly*, May 1981, pp. 30-34.

Sales Representative—For an individual hotel, a sales representative deals with clients to bring meetings or conventions to the hotel. He or she is also heavily involved in public relations work within the community. At the corporate or regional headquarters level, the salesrep deals with airlines and travel agents to bring tours to the hotels in the chain.

The career path for someone beginning in sales or marketing would involve movement between the two areas. A typical path might be Corporate Marketing Analyst, to individual property Sales Representative, to Sales Director, to Regional Sales or Marketing Staff, to the corporate office again as either Vice-President of Sales or Marketing.

The position of General Manager of a property is most often reached, for the MBA, through sales/marketing. The typical path might be entry-level sales or marketing position to Assistant Manager to Rooms Manager to Operations Manager to General Manager. The cross-functional training from marketing to several line management positions provides the necessary training for General Manager. Further upward movement, if desired, would be to Regional Manager for many properties and from there to corporate staff in various top executive positions.

The General Manager position might appeal to those with entrepreneurial interests for it is the General Manager who oversees several hundred people and greatly affects the atmosphere, personality, and profitability of the individual hotel.

Entry Level in Corporate Planning

Corporate Planning Analyst—An Analyst is essentially an internal consultant who does project evaluations in all sectors of hotel operations. This area allows the trainee to become familiar with all phases of the company, but it is a staff position and as such it has no direct effect on the hotel's operations. The most likely career path for an analyst would be to move up within the planning area, perhaps to Vice-President of Planning.

The skills learned from the large hotel chains are highly marketable within the industry. It is more difficult, however, to move from a small hotel to the large ones because of the differences in management policies and procedures.

Some Employers

Full-Service Hotels

Hilton Hotels Corporation (Beverly Hills, California)
Holiday Inn, Inc. (Memphis, Tennessee)
Howard Johnsons, Inc. (Boston, Massachusetts)
Hyatt Hotels, Inc. (Chicago, Illinois)
Marriott Corporation (Bethesda, Maryland)
Olympic Hotel (Seattle, Washington)

Sheraton Corporation (Boston, Massachusetts)
Sonesta International Hotels Corp. (Boston, Massachusetts)

Budget Hotels

Days Inns of America, Inc. (Atlanta, Georgia)
Quality Inns International, Inc. (Silver Spring, Maryland)

Sources of Additional Information

Hotel and Motel Management magazine.

30   INSURANCE

INTRODUCTION

The insurance industry, like other financial industries with fiduciary responsibilities, has been traditionally very conservative. This conservatism generally spills over into insurance organizations making them more sedate than many hard-charging, ambitious MBAs would like. Some firms, however, have been very creative and aggressive, further pointing up the value of searching within industries for organizational characteristics that fit one's personal profile and preferences.

There are several major chunks identified separately by employees in the industry. These include the Casualty, Fire and Marine, Personal Lines, Life, and Group categories. The customers, methods of doing business, and structure of products varies significantly from one category to the next.

We take a functional approach to the industry here, outlining opportunities in investment management, strategic planning, market research, product management, and sales and brokerage. You can construct a grid with these functional areas running down one axis and the categories listed above running along the other axis. Each intersecting cell then suggests a career opportunity that can be explored all within the insurance industry.

INSURANCE: INVESTMENT MANAGEMENT

Education (degrees)	BA	MBA	PhD
Experience required (yrs)	None	1-3	3+
Location	Urban	Rural	Regional / Travel
Compensation ($/yr)	< $25K	$25-30K	$30-35K / >$35K
Work involvement (hrs/wk)	< 50	50-60	> 60
Pace	Relaxed	Medium	Frenetic
Career path (a la Driver)	Spiral	Steady	Linear
Interpersonal style	Loner	Moderate	Outgoing
Cognitive style	Sequential Rules Details	Mixed Principles Systems	Random Free form Big picture
Variety (preference for)	No change Ordered	Occasional Change	Ambiguous Changing

Job Description/Typical Day

MBAs enter the financial area of insurance as Junior Investment Analysts. Analysts read financial news constantly and research companies to buy their stock or loan them money. Within a few years, Junior Analysts are promoted to Senior Analysts and act as resources to others based on their knowledge of particular industries. After this, Analysts become Investment Managers where they head a team of analysts and have decision-making authority for investments. For more information on the skills, compensation, and career paths of Investment Managers, see Investment Management (Section 33).

Other opportunities are available in financial research, where analysts review capital structure and long-term finance options.

INSURANCE: STRATEGIC PLANNING

Job Description/Typical Day

The duties of the Strategic Planners are similar to those of the financial analysts, with a focus on long-term potential areas of investment. Planners also analyze the balance of asset deployment within the company.

Typical Career Path

MBAs in planning are not on the fast track. They move in their staff function from Researchers to Research Team Heads, eventually to Director of Corporate Planning. They can later transfer to other planning jobs for different firms or go into consulting.

For additional information on the skills and compensation of Planners, see Corporate Planning (Section 8).

INSURANCE: MARKET RESEARCH

	BA	MBA	PhD
Education (degrees)	BA	MBA	PhD
Experience required (yrs)	None	1-3	3+
Location	Urban	Rural	Regional / Travel
Compensation ($/yr)	< $25K	$25-30K	$30-35K / >$35K
Work involvement (hrs/wk)	< 50	50-60	> 60
Pace	Relaxed	Medium	Frenetic
Career path (a la Driver)	Spiral	Steady	Linear
Interpersonal style	Loner	Moderate	Outgoing
Cognitive style	Sequential Rules Details	Mixed Principles Systems	Random Free form Big picture
Variety (preference for)	No change Ordered	Occasional Change	Ambiguous Changing

Job Description/Typical Day

The duties of Market Researchers include evaluation of product performance, go/no-go product decisions, market analysis, customer segmentation, and promotional strategies.

Skills

Market Researchers require analytical, number-crunching skills. They also need interpersonal skills in dealing with their research teams and for successfully carrying out their research.

Compensation

Typically, it runs between $25,000 and $30,000.

Typical Career Paths

MBAs in market research start as Researchers, but their proven analytical capabilities speed their promotion to Research Team Managers. A Researcher can move to other research jobs or, what is more likely, into product management.

INSURANCE: PRODUCT MANAGEMENT

Education (degrees)	BA	MBA	PhD
Experience required (yrs)	None	1-3	3+
Location	Urban	Rural	Regional / Travel
Compensation ($/yr)	$< \$25K$	$25-30K	$30-35K / $>\$35K$
Work involvement (hrs/wk)	< 50	50-60	> 60
Pace	Relaxed	Medium	Frenetic
Career path (a la Driver)	Spiral	Steady	Linear
Interpersonal style	Loner	Moderate	Outgoing
Cognitive style	Sequential Rules Details	Mixed Principles Systems	Random Free form Big picture
Variety (preference for)	No change Ordered	Occasional Change	Ambiguous Changing

Job Description/Typical Day

Product management in insurance patterns the typical consumer product career path. (See Product Management.) MBAs begin as Product Assistants developing market plans and monitoring implementation of earlier plans. MBAs become Product Managers within three years, coordinating the marketing plan with the other corporate functional areas. Product Managers can transfer to other marketing jobs in service industries.

INSURANCE: SALES AND BROKERAGE

Education (degrees)	BA	MBA	PhD
Experience required (yrs)	None	1-3	3+
Location	Urban	Rural	Regional / Travel
Compensation ($/yr)	< $25K	$25-30K	$30-35K / >$35K
Work involvement (hrs/wk)	< 50	50-60	> 60
Pace	Relaxed	Medium	Frenetic
Career path (a la Driver)	Spiral	Steady	Linear
Interpersonal style	Loner	Moderate	Outgoing
Cognitive style	Sequential Rules Details	Mixed Principles Systems	Random Free form Big picture
Variety (preference for)	No change Ordered	Occasional Change	Ambiguous Changing

Job Description/Typical Day

Nontraditional positions for MBAs include insurance sales and brokerage. Insurance sales can be as unsophisticated as debit sales, where the agent collects insurance premiums throughout a specific territory, or as complex as designing and underwriting a flexible benefits package for a *Fortune* 500 company. Insurance Salespeople prospect, solicit, sell, and maintain clients by determining their insurance needs, convincing them of those needs, and properly servicing their policies. Agents work unusual hours, at the convenience of their clients, and travel extensively (though locally).

Insurance Brokers work with representatives of many companies to help them find the most suitable coverage; they act as the intermediaries between the consumer and the insurance agents. Brokers' hours are more regular, but they also travel and entertain extensively.

Skills

Insurance sales requires excellent interpersonal skills, for this is very much a "people" business. It also requires persistence, aggressiveness, stamina, and a goal orientation. Brokers need analytical ability to judge the relative merits of different policies for their client and interpersonal skills to deal effectively with client and agent.

Compensation

Insurance Agents are paid minimal salaries (or expense accounts) by their companies. Their income is earned through commissions on the policies they sell. MBAs should, therefore, expect very little income for a period of six months to a year as they begin to build their client base. After that, the income potential is unlimited. The top insurance agents make well into the six figures.

Brokers also earn much of their income through commissions; however, some work on a flat-fee basis for their clients.

Typical Career Paths

The career path of Agents and Brokers is a steady state; that is, there is no vertical advancement. The exceptions to this are those Agents who prefer sales management to direct sales. Sales Managers receive an override on the commissions earned by their agents.

Some Employers

The ten largest insurance companies, as of the 1980 ranking, are:

Aetna Life (Hartford, Connecticut)
Connecticut General (Bloomfield, Connecticut)

Equitable Life Assurance (New York, New York)
John Hancock (Boston, Massachusetts)
Metropolitan (New York, New York)
New York Life (New York, New York)
Northwestern Mutual (Milwaukee, Wisconsin)
Prudential (Newark, New Jersey)
Teachers Insurance & Annuity (New York, New York)
Travelers (Hartford, Connecticut)

Sources of Additional Information

Institutional Investor
Insurance Almanac
Insurance Marketing
Journal of Risk and Insurance
Risk Management
Who's Who in Insurance

31   INTERNATIONAL BANKING

INTRODUCTION

International banking opportunities for MBAs usually include two main areas: lending or credit and operations. The former is primarily concerned with the evaluation of credit requests and decision making on those requests. Lending in the international arena requires a deep and current knowledge of international financial patterns, cultures, and transactions; a facility with people of widely divergent values and perspectives, and an ability to mobilize both rationally and emotionally disparate resources within the home institution. Operations relates to the flow of funds and transactions within the bank that services the credits already established. Both activities are essential to successful international banking: the former requires more customer contact and financial understanding, and the latter requires more ability to manage people and systems to produce desired results. We will only outline the lending job here.

INTERNATIONAL LENDING

	BA	MBA	PhD
Education (degrees)	BA	MBA	PhD
Experience required (yrs)	None	1-3	3+
Location	Urban	Rural	Regional / Travel
Compensation ($/yr)	< $25K	$25-30K	$30-35K / >$35K
Work involvement (hrs/wk)	< 50	50-60	> 60
Pace	Relaxed	Medium	Frenetic
Career path (a la Driver)	Spiral	Steady	Linear
Interpersonal style	Loner	Moderate	Outgoing
Cognitive style	Sequential Rules Details	Mixed Principles Systems	Random Free form Big picture
Variety (preference for)	No change Ordered	Occasional Change	Ambiguous Changing

Job Description/Typical Day

MBAs beginning in the International division of a major money center bank will typically be required to work through a training program their first one to twelve months of work. These training programs range in variety from spreading financial statements* of customers over and over again for months on end to highly varied training and experiential exercises in various parts of the bank (intended to familiarize the Trainee with the bank's operations flow and the personnel who work in various departments: skill in managing those flows and people is essential to the job later on). A typical day will vary considerably during the more varied training programs. By the end of the training program, the Trainee is usually the topic of conversation among various department heads, and those conversations usually lead to an invitation to join an area. Do not assume that completion of the training program assures you of a job. Wise Trainees will begin building relationships with lending officers in various departments well before they finish the training program.

Once a person is assigned to an area, say, the Far East Area, and receives a desk and a portfolio of accounts (perhaps as many as 50 depending on the industry, the structure of the bank, and the size of the customers), a routine sets in that might include the following:

Review the telexes from overseas from the night before. Attend to urgent matters immediately. Some ask for additional information on one of your accounts, others ask for status on a loan request made earlier, others report information you had asked for earlier. Some include financial data on customers. Some report problems with customers either in their long-term business outlook or in current repayment schedules.

Continue working on loan requests for several customers. This includes putting together financial information, spreading it, analyzing, assessing the dependability and viability of the management (often secondhand through the reports of colleagues on site overseas), writing summaries, and making recommendations. This information is collected from published sources, credit files, the credit department, other lending officers, telexes to overseas colleagues, and general knowledge about the economies of the countries involved and of the nature of the business of the clients.

Read through the stack of international trade journals, newspapers, financial newsletters, and articles routed over your desk. This stack may be three or four inches thick daily.

Attend a meeting of the international loan committee, the group of senior colleagues charged with approving or rejecting individual requests. There you will make the case for your credits, often including the weight of the history of the

---

*As each customer's annual financial data become available, the credit files and analysis of each customer must be updated. The new financial data are transferred or "spread" to a form, unique to each bank, that summarizes several years of data.

relationship of the customer with the bank, the financial analysis, the relationship of the current management to the field officer, and your understanding of how this particular credit would fit or not fit into the overall strategy and financial health of the bank. Political considerations in the host country are also of major importance. In this discussion you will be asked many questions depending on the comprehensiveness of your proposal.

In response to a telex regarding a lost payment, you walk across the street or up (or down) three floors to the International Operations department to find out what happened to this particular payment. An intimate knowledge of international financial transactions, including the intricacies of letters of credit, is essential for following and sorting out these conversations and the return letters/telexes you will have to write.

Occasionally, a special project will come along and you may be asked to write a computer program to calculate the effective yield of long-term uneven repayment loans or to recommend changes to the organizational system that ensures that the bank's credit files are up-to-date when any one of the three or more auditing groups (Comptrollers Office, Federal Reserve, State Regulatory agencies, in-house auditors) suddenly, without announcement, appear at the door and ask to see your files.

There is really no one to supervise. Your boss is doing what you are doing. *His* boss is doing what you are doing. His boss is doing what you are doing. All with larger numbers and more sensitive accounts, but by the first year, you are doing what bankers do.

Skills

You need a good understanding of international economics, of the effects of political systems on the international monetary system, financial analysis skills, and excellent interpersonal/social skills for the numerous receptions and negotiating sessions that are a central part of international banking. You must also be patient. Few banks in this relatively cautious, fiduciary industry are willing to give lots of financial responsibility and the risk that goes along with it to unseasoned, inexperienced officers. The development of judgment is critical in the eyes of most senior officers.

Compensation

Entry-level banking positions tend to be at or below the average starting salaries for most major business school graduates. Top-tier candidates in New York can start at $35,000 while the same candidate on the West Coast may receive $5,000 to $10,000 less because of the desirability of living in California and the cost-of-living differential. Salaries over the course of the career tend to lag the more risky, entrepreneurial occupations, but in return, most banks are more loathe to fire someone than many other industries. Medical, dental, and other kinds of insurance and benefits are usually meager. Some banks have retirement plans that vest after five years; others offer stock purchase options.

Typical Career Paths

Trainee–International Lending Officer–Assistant Vice-President–Vice President–Senior Vice-President–Executive Vice-President–President is a common pattern of rank titles. One may receive different assignments along the way, spending a year or two in personnel, in marketing, or some other staff position in the bank. International banking usually requires several years of residence overseas, as well, often in two- to five-year chunks in different parts of the globe. Banks that capitalize on individual backgrounds make a greater effort to match individuals with indicated parts of the globe and tend not to dilute those skills by transferring those persons to other regions unless a broadening perspective is needed in anticipation of further promotion. An officer may be sent overseas immediately, or not for several years. This is a matter that should receive careful attention during the interview process: the criteria including individual performance and the nature of the bank's business and clientele should be thoughtfully sorted out in advance.

Some Employers

Most of the major money center banks have International divisions or groups. The American banks include:

Bankers Trust (New York, New York)
Bank of America (San Francisco, California)
Chase Manhattan (New York, New York)
Citibank (New York, New York)
Continental Illinois (Chicago, Illinois)
First Chicago (Chicago, Illinois)
Manufacturers Hanover (New York, New York)
Marine Midland (Buffalo, New York)
Mellon (Pittsburgh, Pennsylvania)
Morgan Guaranty (New York, New York)
Security Pacific (Los Angeles, California)
Wells Fargo (San Francisco, California)
Western Bancorp (Los Angeles, California)

The international banks may be more difficult in the long run to advance in, but more infrequently they, too, offer American MBAs entry-level positions: Barclays (London), National Westminster (London), Credit Lyonnais (Paris), Banque Nationale de Paris (Paris), and the Deutsche Bank (Frankfurt).

There are a number of less well-known international banks like the European-American Bank that also hire.

Having an international bank telephone number or shingle does not ensure that a bank is committed to its International division. Most banks have flagship divisions, and you should attempt to sort out not only the situation within the International division but also the relative standing of the division within the larger bank. This is important in terms of the quality of talent (colleagues) the International division will attract in the industry, the skill of the people in the division, the availability of resources to the division, and ultimately the working environment in the division.

Sources of Additional Information

See the annual reviews of international banking industry in *Business Week*, *Forbes*, and *Fortune*.

For more information on bank operations, albeit from a domestic side, see the "First National Citibank" case describing the work of John Reed, now the chief executive officer, available from Harvard Case Services, Soldiers Field, Boston, Mass. 02163.

32   INVESTMENT BANKING

INTRODUCTION

Investment Bankers assist clients with major financial transactions such as issuing debt or equity or buying and selling other companies. Most firms divide their investment banking activities into Corporate and Municipal Finance departments. Departmental activities include financial analyses, preparation of documents for the client, and presentations of financing proposals to clients. Younger members of the department may find themselves particularly involved in preparing the analyses and documents for the clients and will be evaluated on their effectiveness in doing this. More senior members are evaluated on their ability to bring new clients to the firm.

    The business is project oriented and paced by frequent deadlines. Hours are very long, and junior department members are often expected to work around the clock when a presentation is in production. Willingness to work long hours and ability to work well in a team are requirements for anyone interested in this field. Travel requirements vary—some Investment Bankers rarely travel; others spend three to four days per week on the road. A career in corporate or municipal finance will generally require residence in or near New York City, since U.S. investment banking activity is concentrated in Manhattan.

    Sales, trading, and arbitrage are also part of a full-service investment banking firm, and MBAs are entering these areas with increasing frequency. These areas are typically characterized by regular hours, little travel, a chaotic working environment, and compensation schedules directly related to one's sales performance.

    We look here at national firms, centered in New York City, and regional firms that provide local, personalized contact with the New York market.

INVESTMENT BANKING: NATIONAL

Education (degrees)	BA	MBA	PhD
Experience required (yrs)	None	1-3	3+
Location	Urban	Rural	Regional / Travel
Compensation ($/yr)	< $25K	$25-30K	$30-35K / >$35K
Work involvement (hrs/wk)	< 50	50-60	> 60
Pace	Relaxed	Medium	Frenetic
Career path (a la Driver)	Spiral	Steady	Linear
Interpersonal style	Loner	Moderate	Outgoing
Cognitive style	Sequential Rules Details	Mixed Principles Systems	Random Free form Big picture
Variety (preference for)	No change Ordered	Occasional Change	Ambiguous Changing

Job Description/Typical Day:

The entry-level position for MBAs entering the corporate finance area of investment banking is as an <u>Associate</u>. The Associate's tasks include financial analysis, preparation of presentations, processing offerings, analysis of potential transactions, and various forms of client contact. The Associate is also the "gofer" for the banking team assigned to a particular project.

The work is often mechanical and detailed. Hours are extremely long (60 to 80 per week), and substantial travel may be required. Despite the long hours, high pressure, and frequent travel, an Investment Banker's life can be described as luxurious in that the firm provides the best possible environment to ensure their employees' maximum productivity. That environment includes first-class travel, frequent client entertainment, and very high remuneration after the first three years.

Skills

The most important skills for this position are interpersonal and financial/analytical. Investment banking requires a certain personality, however; it requires a highly motivated and ambitious (aggressive) person who places work as a top priority and who has high income goals.

Compensation

Compensation systems vary among firms and also from year to year depending on profitability. Most firms stress incentive-based compensation systems with remuneration tied to performance. Compensation is typically salary plus bonus. Bonus size depends on firm, department, and, of course, individual performance. The first- and second-year bonuses range from 10 to 25 percent of base salary. As an Associate progresses with the firm, the bonus increases as a percentage of base salary. Generally, a six-figure income within a five-year period is entirely reasonable. Performance rather than seniority is the principal criterion for advancement. In private firms, election to partnership after eight to ten years is possible. Each Partner is entitled to a share of total earnings; the actual share will depend on the performance and seniority of the Partner. At the Partner level, average earnings can be conservatively estimated at $500,000 for the most profitable firms. Partners are not always allowed to withdraw their full share of earnings in any given year, however, and additional restrictions may exist on a Partner's ability to withdraw capital when leaving the firm. Partnership structure does not exist in publicly held firms. While salaries at the Associate level are fairly uniform across the spectrum of public and private firms, compensation at the senior level may be less in public firms. Officers in public firms, however, generally keep all their compensation. Starting salaries for 1982 ranged between $35,000 and $40,000.

Typical Career Paths

A typical advancement route in corporate finance might be Associate (two to three years), Assistant Vice-President (two to three years), Vice-President (three to four years), Partner. The speed and odds of making Partner, and the levels of responsibility along the way, vary significantly by firm. Public finance, at present, tends to have a faster track, but increasing competition in this area should bring this more into line with the opportunities in corporate finance.

At the partnership level, this is a very flexible industry. As a workaholic you can earn half a million or more per year. As an alternative, you can earn a quarter of a million and accept outside corporate directorships, lead foundations, or enter the realm of politics. One firm said that many partners leave to start their own ventures; others head to Washington. The key to the transferability is contacts developed while part of the industry.

Transferability, especially after five or more years in the business, is relatively low within the firm or outside of the industry, such as into corporations or consulting firms, though it is quite high within the industry (especially if one has gained specialized expertise or makes a lateral move to a smaller firm or a merchant banking group of a commercial bank).

While it would be quite easy to transfer from New York to a regional office or firm, to reverse this would be more difficult.

Reputation of the firm is a critical factor for success in the industry from other firms' viewpoint.

Some Employers

National investment banking firms hire only at the top business schools, and the field is extremely competitive. Most of the large national firms are listed here; headquarters for all are in New York City.

Blythe, Eastman
Dean, Witter, Reynolds
Dillon, Read
Donaldson, Lufkin & Jenrette
First Boston
Goldman, Sachs
E. F. Hutton
Kidder, Peabody
Lehman Brothers
Merrill Lynch
Morgan, Stanley
Salomon Brothers

Additional Information

Job potential in investment banking may be diminishing over the long term due to industry concentration (fewer firms), dependence of industry growth on general economic conditions (which may continue to be poor), and a possible slowing of merger activity among business firms. In addition, many MBAs have been hired by investment banking firms in the past decade, reducing opportunities for new entrants. Public finance is presently growing faster than corporate finance, but this area, too, may slow over the next five years. Sales, trading, and arbitrage potential depend heavily on market conditions; "advancement" in these areas generally takes the form of monetary compensation rather than hierarchical progress.

Note that company cultures differ widely within the industry.

Sources of Additional Information

Finance
Financial Analysts' Journal
Fortune
Institutional Investor

INVESTMENT BANKING: REGIONAL

Education (degrees)	BA	MBA	PhD
Experience required (yrs)	None	1-3	3+
Location	Urban	Rural	Regional / Travel
Compensation ($/yr)	< $25K	$25-30K	$30-35K / >$35K
Work involvement (hrs/wk)	< 50	50-60	> 60
Pace	Relaxed	Medium	Frenetic
Career path (a la Driver)	Spiral	Steady	Linear
Interpersonal style	Loner	Moderate	Outgoing
Cognitive style	Sequential Rules Details	Mixed Principles Systems	Random Free form Big picture
Variety (preference for)	No change Ordered	Occasional Change	Ambiguous Changing

INTRODUCTION

Regional investment banking is an industry of great diversity in terms of size, product mix, organization, number and type of branches, philosophy, and strategy. The regional industry can be defined as consisting of firms headquartered outside of New York City and operating in a limited geographic area rather than maintaining a nationwide branch system. Their revenue base and clientele, however, often are national and international in scope.

The best opportunities for MBAs are in the full-service regional banks, as opposed to the specialized firms that concentrate most of their efforts in a particular facet of the industry. The diversified firms offer services in underwriting, corporate finance, trading, securities analysis, investment management, real estate, venture capital, and brokerage.

Job Description/Typical Day

Corporate Finance is by far the most frequent entry position. In regional investment banking firms, this will include underwriting new equity and debt issues, doing private placements, and offering advisory services to individual and corporate clients. The regional firms' "culture" generally involves less pressure and not as long hours when compared with the large national firms. There will typically be more client contact earlier in the career with a regional firm because of smaller staffs and smaller clients.

Regional firms are seeking individuals with a more entrepreneurial and generalist orientation. Having some local "roots" in the community is also viewed as an asset. Travel will depend on the firm and the position but generally involves a little more time, again due to the smaller staff to cover the clientele. Regionals, particularly the growth firms, are characterized by easier access to senior members in the firm, more cooperation, and less competition than in the national firms.

Skills

See Investment Banking: National (Section 32).

Compensation

Compensation varies widely by firm, as well as by region. Total compensation is usually composed of salary and a bonus. In general, starting salaries with regionals will be less than those of the national firms. (See Investment Banking: National.) After adding in bonuses and adjusting for cost-of-living differentials, however, the regional firms are comparable and often exceed the compensation packages of their national counterparts. The big difference between the national and regional firms in compensation is in the opportunity to participate in equity "deals." These investment opportunties are available much earlier in the regionals and can result in significant capital gains.

Typical Career Paths

The diversity of the regionals makes it again difficult to generalize. For those entering corporate finance, a three-year apprenticeship is most typical before reaching the Assistant Vice-President level, and another four years to reach Vice-President. If the firm is a partnership, ten years would be the average time required to make Partner after receiving an MBA.

If the entry position is in sales, an initial six months will be spent in training to prepare for the registration examination given by New York Stock Exchange and National Association of Stock Dealers. Once the employee becomes registered, he or she will begin to sell. After selling for a minimum of five years, the career path could take several different directions.

Some Employers

The following is a sample of some of the larger and more diversified regional investment banking firms. A good source for names of other firms and the services they offer is Standard & Poor's *Securities Dealers of North America.*

Northeast

Advest Company (Hartford, Connecticut)
F. S. Moseley & Co. (Boston, Massachusetts)
H. C. Wainwright & Co. (Boston, Massachusetts)

Middle Atlantic

Alex Brown (Baltimore, Maryland)
Butcher & Singer (Philadelphia, Pennsylvania)
Drexel, Firestone, Inc. (Philadelphia, Pennsylvania)

Southeast

Howard, Weil, Labouisse, Fredericks, Inc. (New Orleans, Louisiana)
Robinson-Humphrey Co. (Atlanta, Georgia)
Wheat, First Securities, Inc. (Richmond, Virginia)

North Central

William Blair & Co. (Chicago, Illinois)
Dain, Kalman & Quail (Minneapolis, Minnesota)
Hillard, Lyons (Louisville, Kentucky)
Loewi & Co. (Milwaukee, Wisconsin)
The Ohio Co. (Columbus, Ohio)
Piper, Jaffray & Hopwood (Minneapolis, Minnesota)
Prescott, Ball & Turben (Cleveland, Ohio)

Middle West

A. G. Edwards (St. Louis, Missouri)
First Southwest (Dallas, Texas)
Rotan Mosle Inc. (Houston, Texas)

West

Hambrecht & Quist (San Francisco, California)
Robertson, Coleman (San Francisco, California)

Additional Sources of Information

See Investment Banking: National, pp. 208-211.

33 INVESTMENT MANAGEMENT

	BA	MBA	PhD
Education (degrees)	BA	MBA	PhD
Experience required (yrs)	None	1-3	3+
Location	Urban	Rural	Regional / Travel
Compensation ($/yr)	< $25K	$25-30K	$30-35K / >$35K
Work involvement (hrs/wk)	< 50	50-60	> 60
Pace	Relaxed	Medium	Frenetic
Career path (a la Driver)	Spiral	Steady	Linear
Interpersonal style	Loner	Moderate	Outgoing
Cognitive style	Sequential Rules Details	Mixed Principles Systems	Random Free form Big picture
Variety (preference for)	No change Ordered	Occasional Change	Ambiguous Changing

INTRODUCTION

The primary activity of an Investment Manager is to make investment decisions based on the vast quantity of information he or she assimilates. This means combining an understanding of specific industries with a feel for the economy as a whole and the direction in which it is moving. The Investment Manager must read voraciously: newspapers, annual reports, and trade publications. A facility with numbers is important.

Depending on the type of organization the manager works for, he or she may have extensive contact with clients (in an investment advisory capacity) or just be accountable to upper management (e.g., in pension fund). We divide the job here into two parts, Analyst and Client Service Person.

ANALYST

Job Description/Typical Day

The Analyst is assigned to from one to four industries and is responsible for buy/sell recommendations on individual companies within those industries. The job entails interviews with upper management of companies, communication with research analysts outside the firm, contact with government agencies if relevant, and so on. The Analyst makes a judgment of the companies and is evaluated on the basis of how accurate that judgment was as reflected by the stock market. The position is high risk—high reward, requires a lot of independence, and is accorded a fair amount of status within and outside the firm. Work hours and schedules are determined mostly by the individual.

Skills

Analytical skills are obviously of prime importance, followed by the ability to deal with, and draw information from, many people.

CLIENT SERVICES

Job Description/Typical Day

The Client Service Person (CSP) is assigned to several client accounts. At the entry level, the CSP works with portfolio managers and other CSPs. The job of the CSP is to define a client's needs, help to maintain a portfolio that meets those needs, and then report back to the client on the portfolio's performance. The CS position is much more people oriented and is less independent. It is still high risk—the CSP is evaluated on how many clients are gained or lost—but it is a risk based on people skills, not analytical skills. The work hours are somewhat less flexible because the CSP is serving the client. There is less status in the CS position, for the CSP typically deals with the Treasurer or Pension Fund Manager whereas the Analyst might deal with the CEO.

Skills

Interpersonal skills are the most crucial in this position, followed by attention to detail and analytical ability.

The degree to which the Analyst and CSP positions are separate depends on the individual firm. In some firms, these positions are very separate; in others, both are done by one person. The amount of responsibility given to a new person also varies from firm to firm, as does the length of tenure in the entry-level position.

Compensation

Investment management firms pay MBAs "competitive" salaries. One source has indicated that a financial analyst salary range was from $25,000 to $65,000.

Typical Career Paths

If one has extensive experience working in a specific industry, the likely career path would start as a Research Analyst covering that industry. If one has no such experience, then the likely career path would start with an institution that relies on analysis performed by others, for example, pension and mutual funds, banks, and insurance companies.

The primary career moves of an Analyst would be into the research function or portfolio management. CSPs normally move into portfolio management. Investment counseling firms have a fairly flat structure. There are some general management positions beyond Portfolio Manager and Senior Analyst, but there aren't many. There is limited transfer between industries but a fair amount of lateral transfer within the industry.

Some nonfinance companies have in-house Corporate Finance positions or Pension Fund Managers. These positions most often fall under the Financial VP's office. Such a position may allow for more transferability to other industries than would a position with an investment management firm.

Some Employers

Insurance Companies

Aetna Life & Casualty (Hartford, Connecticut)
Connecticut General Life (Bloomfield, Connecticut)
Equitable Life Insurance (New York, New York)
Prudential Life Insurance (Newark, New Jersey)
Travelers (Hartford, Connecticut)

Investment Banking Firms

Paine Webber (New York, New York)
Salomon Brothers (New York, New York)
Wertheim and Company (New York, New York)

Investment Management/Counciling Firms

Dodge and Cox (San Francisco, California)
Investors Diversified Services (Minneapolis, Minnesota)
Loomis and Sayles (Boston, Massachusetts)
Massachusetts Financial Service Co. (Boston, Massachusetts)
Putnam Management Company (Boston, Massachusetts)
T. Rowe Price (Baltimore, Maryland)
Scudder Stevens and Clark (Boston, Massachusetts)
Stein, Roe, Farnham (Chicago, Illinois)
Wellington Management (Valley Forge, Pennsylvania)

Sources of Additional Information

Credit and Financial Management.
Financial World
Institutional Investor
Journal of Financial Analyst
Journal of Portfolio Management
Money Market Directory: Institutional Investors and Their Portfolio Managers
Pension World

34 LEASING

Education (degrees)	BA	MBA	PhD
Experience required (yrs)	None	1-3	3+
Location	Urban	Rural	Regional / Travel
Compensation ($/yr)	< $25K	$25-30K	$30-35K / >$35K
Work involvement (hrs/wk)	< 50	50-60	> 60
Pace	Relaxed	Medium	Frenetic
Career path (a la Driver)	Spiral	Steady	Linear
Interpersonal style	Loner	Moderate	Outgoing
Cognitive style	Sequential Rules Details	Mixed Principles Systems	Random Free form Big picture
Variety (preference for)	No change Ordered	Occasional Change	Ambiguous Changing

INTRODUCTION

Some distinction should be recognized among leasing companies, investment banks, and commercial banks. The investment banks and leasing companies primarily act as agents between investor, or lessor, and lessee. The investor is generally attracted to the terms because of tax benefits. Commercial banks differ because they usually act as lessor to gain the tax benefits for their own organization. The commercial banks, therefore, often have a more limited appetite for lease agreements. In addition, the risk is often reduced by imposing rigid guidelines for the leasing terms.

Job Description/Typical Day

Leasing Companies

Marketer of Financial Services—The function is to provide interface between the customer and the leasing company. The key elements of the job are the design and negotiations of the lease transaction to suit client needs.

Lease Underwriter—This function is to structure the pricing of the transaction, sell the transaction to the investor, and guide the transaction through all stages of documentation and delivery.

Commercial Bank

Leasing Officer—This function serves as marketer of financial services as well as structures and agreements to the client's needs.

Leasing is transaction oriented and requires development and completion of an entire project. Time required varies from firm to firm. Investment banks are the most demanding. Leasing firms and commercial banks are demanding, but long hours are not required to be successful.

Skills

Leasing requires skills in analyzing complex economic and tax considerations to generate minimum cost to the client and highest yield to the firm. Understanding of specific customer needs is essential. One must have skill in sophisticated financial management and be able to keep track of and anticipate changing conditions.

In addition to analytical skills, it is also essential to have strong interpersonal skills, particularly the ability to supply a clear and comprehensive explanation of the leasing terms. Sales skills are essential to completing the deal.

Compensation

Excellent compensation can be earned for performers. Most organizations compensate with a salary-plus-bonus system. The bonus is formulated with respect to volume of leases as well as yield of the lease agreements.

Typical Career Paths

In leasing companies the entry-level position can lead to opportunities in general management for the whole organization, whereas in commercial banks it can lead only to management within the leasing division. Getting into general bank management requires going outside the leasing function.

From the outset, either type of organization delegates responsibility quickly. Acquiring a solid understanding of the leasing business usually requires two to three years of experience.

Some Employers

Leasing Companies

GATX (Chicago, Illinois)
G.E. Credit Corporation (New York, New York)
U.S. Leasing International (San Francisco, California)

Commercial Banks

Bank Amerilease Group (Los Angeles, California)
Chemlease Worldwide (New York, New York)

Investment Banks

Goldman, Sachs (New York, New York)
Kidder, Peabody (New York, New York)
Merrill Lynch (New York, New York)

Insurance Companies

Aetna (Hartford, Connecticut)
Equitable (Hartford, Connecticut)
Metropolitan (New York, New York)
Prudential (Newark, New Jersey)

Almost all investment banks and commercial banks have a lease group, but emphasis on this function varies from firm to firm.

Additional Information

In July 1981, President Reagan's tax policy implemented a number of significant changes for leasing. This change has made leasing increasingly attractive for both the lessee and lessor. In response to this, leasing firms have moved to increase their activities, making this an industry with increasing opportunity.

Sources of Additional Information

Pension World
Money

35 OIL

Education (degrees)	BA	MBA	PhD
Experience required (yrs)	None	1-3	3+
Location	Urban	Rural	Regional / Travel
Compensation ($/yr)	$< $25K$	$25-30K	$30-35K / $>$35K
Work involvement (hrs/wk)	< 50	50-60	> 60
Pace	Relaxed	Medium	Frenetic
Career path (a la Driver)	Spiral	Steady	Linear
Interpersonal style	Loner	Moderate	Outgoing
Cognitive style	Sequential Rules Details	Mixed Principles Systems	Random Free form Big picture
Variety (preference for)	No change Ordered	Occasional Change	Ambiguous Changing

Job Description/Typical Day

Entry-level jobs are usually staff or planning jobs. Staff Analyst jobs are available in Finance, Marketing, Controller's, Transportation, Refining, and many other departments. Typical assignments include earnings analysis, cost analysis, sales trend analysis, lease versus purchase, and so on. These types of assignments are fairly common regardless of the department chosen. Most firms also have corporate planning groups with openings for MBAs. A technical background is required for entry-level positions in operations.

The daily routine in most entry-level jobs involves little travel in general, but there are significant exceptions between companies and departments within companies. As advancement occurs, travel can increase significantly, especially in operations. Average to long hours are the norm for most MBAs. Job changes are fairly rapid and are quite often accompanied by transfers.

Skills

Quantitative skills are very important. Communication skills and the ability to get along with people are, as usual, considered critical.

Compensation

The following is a profile of Harvard 1980 graduates who entered the oil industry.

Salary

Range:	$26,000–59,000
Mean:	$33,183
Median:	$30,750

Employer Size

Large	75.0%
Medium	8.3%
Small	16.7%

Undergraduate Degrees

Business	25.0%
Technical	58.3%
Social Science	16.7%

Positions Taken

General management	4
Project management	2
Planning	2
Marketing	2
Production	2
Finance	4
Accounting	4
	20

Benefits

Employees enjoy full range of insurance benefits. Perks are widespread. First-class treatment for executives.

Typical Career Paths

Those with nontechnical degrees go into planning, finance, marketing, or transportation while those with technical degrees often go into line management positions in operating divisions.

There is little mobility between functions. Normally you will stay in one function during your entire career. Once you reach the top of your specialty, you will receive exposure to other functions. One advantage of the planning function is that it cuts across the functional boundaries in the organization and gives you a broader perspective.

Tenure in the original staff positions usually is two or three years. First-line supervision usually occurs after three to five years. When describing career paths in the oil industry, *variety* is the key word. Job assignments are extremely diverse, and no "typical" career path exists. Movement between functions and departments is common, and flexibility is very important. In technical areas, project management jobs are common. Some type of operations experience is very important for progression to top management.

A technical background is important for promotion to upper management, and companies find ways and opportunities to provide adequate operations experience to nontechnical managers. There are no "fast-track" programs for MBAs.

There is no consistent industry pattern of training programs. Types of programs vary depending on the firm and the department.

Because of the breadth of experience available in the oil industry, the management skills acquired are easily transferable to other industries.

Some Employers

Virtually all the large oil companies have openings for MBA grads. Increasingly, the independents are hiring MBAs as well. At present, industry experience is preferred, but entry-level jobs in financial analysis are becoming common in these smaller companies.

The number of graduates hired varies greatly among firms. Exxon hired 150 new MBAs in 1979, Mobil hired 60, and Arco hired 20.

Sources of Additional Information

Coal Age
Fuel Oil, Oil Heat and Solar Systems
Oil and Gas Journal

36 PUBLIC ACCOUNTING

Education (degrees)	BA	MBA	PhD
Experience required (yrs)	None	1-3	3+
Location	Urban	Rural	Regional / Travel
Compensation ($/yr)	< $25K	$25-30K	$30-35K / >$35K
Work involvement (hrs/wk)	< 50	50-60	> 60
Pace	Relaxed	Medium	Frenetic
Career path (a la Driver)	Spiral	Steady	Linear
Interpersonal style	Loner	Moderate	Outgoing
Cognitive style	Sequential Rules Details	Mixed Principles Systems	Random Free form Big picture
Variety (preference for)	No change Ordered	Occasional Change	Ambiguous Changing

Job Description/Typical Day

Initial assignments of a <u>Staff Accountant</u> include examination of control systems and financial records of a variety of types and sizes of companies. The review of financial information systems is designed to appraise their effectiveness in order to determine the scope of the verification work required of the accounting firm. The primary purpose of auditing is to judge the accuracy and fairness of financial statements. Initial assignments are generally designed to offer experience in different industries and can be structured to meet individual preferences.

Skills

The key skill required is demonstrated financial analytical aptitude, followed by an attention to detail. Organizational skills are also important. CPA status is not required immediately, but a minimum number of accounting courses are necessary as is a definite plan for taking the requisite courses at a local university.

Compensation

Compensation varies primarily according to the experience of the applicant. Traditionally, accounting firms have started at low salaries compared with comparable corporate positions. Here is one CPA's estimate of the salary structure for an MBA in accounting:

Starting salary	$20,000
Two years later	25,000
Five years later	32,000
Ten years later	60,000

Typical Career Path

Within an accounting firm, specialization is usually possible in at least four major areas: tax, small business, management advisory services, and audit. Audit is the largest area, small business is the newest, and management advisory services is the fastest growing. (See Section 22 on Consulting for information regarding management advisory services.)

Generally, promotion is based on technical competence, good client relations, and successful project completion within budget and at acceptable quality levels. The career path proceeds from Junior to Senior Staff, then Manager, then Partner. Partners report to managing partners or to the directors of functional specialists.

Following initial work experience in a public accounting firm, many accountants transfer to companies where they can assume positions such as audit manager, general accounting manager, or other finance positions. Both of the former positions report to a Controller, Treasurer, or Vice-President of Finance.

Some Employers

The accounting firms referred to as the "Big Eight" are:

Arthur Anderson & Co. (Chicago, Illinois)
Coopers & Lybrand (New York, New York)
Deloitte, Haskins & Sells (New York, New York)
Ernst & Whinney (Cleveland, Ohio)
Peat, Marwick & Mitchell (New York, New York)
Price Waterhouse (New York, New York)
Touche Ross and Co (New York, New York)
Arthur Young and Co. (New York, New York)

Other major employers include:

Financial Accounting Standards Board (Stamford, Connecticut)
Alexander Grant & Co. (Chicago, Illinois)
Institute of Internal Auditors (Altamonte Springs, Florida)
Laventhol Krekstein Horwath and Horwath (Philadelphia, Pennsylvania)
Oppenheim, Appel, Dixon and Company (New York, New York)

Additional Information

The demand for qualified accounting graduates by public accounting firms is expected to be greater than the supply for the foreseeable future due to (1) the need for more efficient audits, (2) more in-depth evaluation of client internal controls, (3) more statistical sampling and electronic data processing, and (4) more direct involvement with clients by higher-level personnel. However, high personnel turnover rates have plagued public accounting firms as a result of outside opportunities in companies for trained professionals and a lack of job satisfaction among employees. MBAs do not feel rewarded for advanced degrees, although job satisfaction increases as employees advance. According to a survey in the *Journal of Accountancy*, August 1981,[1] the most troublesome areas were recognition for a job well done, need for firm policy and administration, recognition of contribution to society, and feedback on performance. Accountancy has been perceived as a low-value-added job, where replacement is easy at the lower levels and salaries are not commensurate with the effort demanded. However, there are signs that this is beginning to change.

With the lifting of bans in 1978 and 1979 on advertising and on direct solicitation of other firms' clients, accounting firms are becoming increasingly marketing oriented. This trend is expected to continue, especially for middle-market companies. Specialized services, such as management consulting, will be

[1]Albrecht, Steve; Brown, Scott W.; and Field, David R., "Toward Increased Job Satisfaction of Practicing CPAs," *Journal of Accountancy*, August 1981, pp. 61-65.

offered to complement the accounting services and provide one-stop financial shopping.

Sources of Additional Information

ABRAHAM, STANLEY C. *The Public Accounting Profession: Problems and Prospects*, Lexington, Massachusetts: Lexington Books, 1978.

CARMICHAEL, D. R., AND J. J. WILLINGHAM. *Perspectives in Auditing*, New York: McGraw-Hill, 1979.

CASHIN, JAMES A., AND D. E. MEYER, eds. *Current Problems in the Accounting Profession*, Hempstead, New York: Hofstra University, 1979.

CPA Journal

Journal of Accountancy

37   PUBLISHING

INTRODUCTION

The publishing industry includes two major sections, one involving the publication of books, the other of periodicals. Both segments of the industry include an array of management functions, with very different areas of required expertise. These areas include circulation, financial, editorial, advertisement, and administrative management. In the book publishing industry, activities lean more toward the editorial, with selection and cultivation of authors from "outside" the company more important. The business side of the book industry has been described as more akin to "deal making": deals with authors, deals for paperback rights, deals for movies, deals for promotion, and the like. The emphasis is to assure that the book selected by the editorial staff, when published, will turn a profit for the company.

The emphasis in the magazine segment of the industry is more heavily placed upon administration in that the ongoing nature of the publication requires active management of circulation rates and, thereby, of advertising revenue. This may be done by stringent literary requirements *(The New Yorker, The Atlantic Monthly,* etc.) or otherwise "targeting" an audience (sports enthusiasts, interior designers, etc.). Other standard product management concerns—in controlling cost of production—have been very important of late, most particularly for the magazine industry because of rising costs of paper and postage.

PUBLISHING: MAGAZINE ADVERTISING DIRECTOR

Education (degrees)	BA	MBA	PhD
Experience required (yrs)	None	1-3	3+
Location	Urban	Rural	Regional / Travel
Compensation ($/yr)	< $25K	$25-30K	$30-35K / >$35K
Work involvement (hrs/wk)	< 50	50-60	> 60
Pace	Relaxed	Medium	Frenetic
Career path (a la Driver)	Spiral	Steady	Linear
Interpersonal style	Loner	Moderate	Outgoing
Cognitive style	Sequential Rules Details	Mixed Principles Systems	Random Free form Big picture
Variety (preference for)	No change Ordered	Occasional Change	Ambiguous Changing

Job Description/Typical Day

Leonard Mogel, Adjunct Professor of Publishing at New York University and publisher of *National Lampoon Magazine*, provides this informative description of the Magazine Advertising Director's job in his book, *The Magazine: Everything You Need to Know to Make It in the Magazine Business:*

> This important individual, usually the number-two person in the department, reporting directly to the publisher, directs all advertising sales on a magazine and is, therefore, responsible for the salespeople, branch-office operations, and out-of-town representatives as well as the back-up staff that generates the promotion, research, and data necessary to make sales happen.
>
> A magazine will often advertise to the trade. That is, it will run ads in publications such as *Advertising Age, Media Decisions*, or *Madison Avenue* in order to sell ad agencies and clients. The creative material for these ads and the budget selection for the campaign is the province of the advertising director, with major decisions subject to the approval of the publisher.
>
> On a day-to-day basis the advertising director will perform a variety of functions, which include key sales calls with the salespeople, developing sales strategy for new business, and analyzing call reports submitted weekly by the house staff and the branch offices.
>
> The advertising director also evaluates research and meets with his or her own staff to discuss problem areas, such as how to break into new product classifications or how to cover an industry convention, or how to plan coordination of the efforts of the home-office salespeople and the out-of-town representatives.
>
> The advertising director also consults with editors concerning future editorial tie-ins. He or she will also direct the creation of sales promotion material relating to the sales of advertising. In this respect, he or she will meet with the sales promotion manager, exchange ideas, and then approve copy and layouts before this material is printed.
>
> This position on the business side of a magazine is a demanding one, highly coveted, and well paid. On even a small magazine, an advertising director will be paid about $30,000 to $35,000 a year. This figure can reach $75,000 to $100,000 on a major publication.[1]

Compensation

Most likely, starting salaries are $25,000 to $30,000. Following a training/indoctrination period of six months or so, a commission incentive is generally added.

Typical Career Paths

The most likely route to the Advertising Manager job is through a position on the sales staff in an industry or trade publication (as opposed to a consumer-oriented magazine). Although technically a sales position, it requires one to be as familiar with the advertisers and their markets as those on the editorial staff.

An Advertising Space Salesperson spends a great deal of time on the phone

---

[1]Mogel, Leonard, *The Magazine: Everything You Need to Know to Make It in the Magazine Business,* Englewood Cliffs, New Jersey: Prentice-Hall, 1979, p. 18.

and frequently visits the offices of the potential advertisers. As one develops a group of customers, the calls and visits become less frequent but last longer because of more detailed discussion of the business.

Intermediate positions between the Ad Sales job and Ad Director would be called Marketing Manager or Marketing Director. These would depend on the size of the magazine.

From the Marketing Manager position, if one didn't desire to be Ad Director, he or she could move on to an upper-level editorial position.

Some Employers

Likely employers are companies such as McGraw-Hill (New York, New York), Fairchild Publications (New York, New York), and Hearst Publications (New York, New York), or other publishers of a great variety of magazines for many different markets.

Sources of Additional Information

BENJAMIN, CURTIS G. *A Candid Critique of Book Publishing*, New York: R.R. Bowker Co., 1977.

BINGLEY, CLIVE. *The Business of Book Publishing*, Oxford, New York: Pergamon Press, 1973.

The Business of Publishing: A PW Anthology, New York: R.R. Bowker Co., 1976.

The Bowker Annual of Library and Book Trade Information, New York: R.R. Bowker Co.

MOGEL, LEONARD. *The Magazine: Everything You Need to Know to Make It in the Magazine Business*, Englewood Cliffs, New Jersey: Prentice-Hall, 1979.

RANKIN, WILLIAM. P. *Business Management of General Consumer Magazines*, New York: Praeger Publications, 1980.

MIMP: Magazine Industry Market Place

PUBLISHING: NEWSPAPERS

	BA	MBA	PhD
Education (degrees)	BA	MBA	PhD
Experience required (yrs)	None	1-3	3+
Location	Urban	Rural	Regional / Travel
Compensation ($/yr)	< $25K	$25-30K	$30-35K / >$35K
Work involvement (hrs/wk)	< 50	50-60	> 60
Pace	Relaxed	Medium	Frenetic
Career path (a la Driver)	Spiral	Steady	Linear
Interpersonal style	Loner	Moderate	Outgoing
Cognitive style	Sequential Rules Details	Mixed Principles Systems	Random Free form Big picture
Variety (preference for)	No change Ordered	Occasional Change	Ambiguous Changing

INTRODUCTION

MBAs entering the newspaper industry will find it becoming increasingly sophisticated as it struggles to overcome rapidly rising costs. Intense competition for increases in circulation and advertising revenues makes the need for effective cost control and careful financial planning even more critical. Newspapers unable to survive this competition are being acquired by large national chains (e.g., the *Denver Post* acquired by Times-Mirror Co.). Further, these large newspaper chains are diversifying into other communications-related businesses, primarily in television stations and cable franchises. These trends might signal an imminent growth in demand for MBAs, especially in finance and control, advertising and sales management, and strategic and corporate development. Maybe.

Newspapers today, however, are still relatively cool to MBAs. This may be related to the historical schism between the editorial and business functions within the average newspaper, comparable to the proverbial separation of church and state. Newspapers must balance the fourth estate's mission to serve and inform the public with the more practical economic imperative to turn a profit. These sometimes conflicting goals make the role of the General Manager in journalism a particularly exciting one, integrating these highly differentiated functions and perspectives into one, profitable, publicly responsible newspaper.

Job Description/Typical Day

The MBA appears to be a weak credential for entry into the editorial side; there is no shortage of talented business writers. Entry-level jobs are more commonly found in functional specialties in the business side, with about half of all jobs in general or project management and the remainder primarily in finance, marketing, and sales/circulation. In most newspapers, circulation is considered the "fast track" by which most General Managers rose to their positions.

Yet, perhaps in response to a perceived need for more professional General Managers in this industry, many newspapers have established small training programs to develop these human resources. We were able to obtain the following information on the training programs of three potential employers:

The New York Times—Small general manager training program, 18 months to 2 years, as Assistant to General Manager.

Capital Cities Communications (New York)—Starting at Corporate Headquarters, work for the President in internal consulting projects. After 2 years, if invited by line manager, transfer to line; otherwise terminated.

Boston Globe—Executive training program develops managers from within. MBA is not a criterion; there are no special programs for MBAs.

Skills

The companies that do recruit MBAs seem to want experience in the communications field, analytical skills, and an appreciation of the press's role in a democratic society. They also stress the willingness to relocate, as many firms consider placing the MBAs in their smaller units outside the New York area. Nonetheless, most jobs *are* in New York and in other big cities.

Compensation

Given the difficulty of finding a job in journalism, companies seem to offer relatively low average salaries in the belief that the MBA seeking to work for a newspaper must be motivated primarily by a love for the business. According to one summer MBA intern at *The New York Times*, most MBAs there are paid in the 20s to start, with the highest salary at about $34,000. This fits with the range of salaries reported by Darden's 1984 class taking jobs in printing and publishing—$18,000 to $38,000.

Some Employers

Potential employers in newspapers and magazines are:

ABC Publishing (New York, New York)
Capital Cities Communications (New York, New York)
CBS Publications (New York, New York)
Chicago Tribune (Chicago, Illinois)
Dow Jones (WSJ) (New York, New York)
Knight-Ridder (Miami, Florida)
Newsweek (New York, New York)
New York Times (New York, New York)
Time (New York, New York)
Times-Mirror (Los Angeles, California)
Washington Post (Washington, D.C.)

Additional Information

Students interested in careers in journalism should expect a job search of greater than average difficulty, requiring initiative and perseverance. If our industry analysis is correct, the effort could pay off, handsomely, in the not-too-distant future.

Sources of Additional Information

Editor and Publisher magazine.
Current industry employees

38 REAL ESTATE

INTRODUCTION

Jobs within the real estate industry can differ greatly with respect to product, service, or geographic region within the following areas: residential, commercial, recreational, shopping centers, food chains, retail, land. Three major areas with opportunities for MBAs are corporate staff positions, such as financial or marketing analyst; project management; and commercial, industrial, or residential brokerage.

Roughly half of the job descriptions for these types of jobs posted at Harvard in 1980 indicated a preference for experience in real estate, engineering, architecture, construction, accounting, law, or real estate case work. (In about half of these postings, these backgrounds were listed as preferences not as requisites.) The other half of the job descriptions did not specify any required background.

Personal traits mentioned in the descriptions include entrepreneurial approach, motivated achiever, strong interpersonal skills, facility with numbers, negotiating skills, assertiveness, creativity, hard driving personality, a detail orientation, and a willingness to relocate.

Jobs more closely related to the entrepreneurial end (developers) are more affected by the cyclicality of the industry. Service businesses that are more diversified and institutions, such as commercial banks and insurance companies, are less likely to cut back personnel in an economic downturn; however, the potential monetary rewards are not as great.

Sensitivity to cycles can be minimized by selection of a job area generally (commercial has been less affected than residential development in recent years) and geographic selection (the Sunbelt has fared better than has the North Central United States). Conditions in a local market (e.g., possible overbuilding in Dallas) should be understood, since they can have as much impact as the *macro* economic forces such as interest rates, the rate of inflation and growth in GNP.

Mobility within the real estate industry, among developers, brokers, consultants, financial institutions, and so on, is relatively easy, although with possible geographic constraints. The major problem is transferability *out* of the industry, which is a difficult task.

REAL ESTATE: STAFF FUNCTIONS

	BA	MBA	PhD
Education (degrees)	BA	MBA	PhD
Experience required (yrs)	None	1-3	3+
Location	Urban	Rural	Regional / Travel
Compensation ($/yr)	$< $25K$	$25-30K	$30-35K / $>$35K
Work involvement (hrs/wk)	< 50	50-60	> 60
Pace	Relaxed	Medium	Frenetic
Career path (a la Driver)	Spiral	Steady	Linear
Interpersonal style	Loner	Moderate	Outgoing
Cognitive style	Sequential Rules Details	Mixed Principles Systems	Random Free form Big picture
Variety (preference for)	No change Ordered	Occasional Change	Ambiguous Changing

238

Job Description/Typical Day

MBAs entering the real estate industry in staff positions usually begin as Assistants-to or Financial or Marketing Analysts. Their duties are similar to those of other corporate analysts and include market studies of real estate demand and capacity, geographic growth trends, competitive moves, project feasibility studies, and financing recommendations and arrangements.

The hours worked and degree of responsibility vary with the size and function of each employer. Corporate staff positions are less affected by the industry cyclicality than are project management and brokerage positions.

Skills

Staff positions require analytical and interpersonal skills. In addition, the applicant must have a commitment to the industry.

Typical Career Paths

The MBA will progress within his or her functional areas and will be assigned to increasingly large and complex project teams. The intermediate end result would be to become a functional Vice-President.

REAL ESTATE: PROJECT MANAGER

Education (degrees)	BA	MBA	PhD
Experience required (yrs)	None	1-3	3+
Location	Urban	Rural	Regional / Travel
Compensation ($/yr)	< $25K	$25-30K	$30-35K / >$35K
Work involvement (hrs/wk)	< 50	50-60	> 60
Pace	Relaxed	Medium	Frenetic
Career path (a la Driver)	Spiral	Steady	Linear
Interpersonal style	Loner	Moderate	Outgoing
Cognitive style	Sequential Rules Details	Mixed Principles Systems	Random Free form Big picture
Variety (preference for)	No change Ordered	Occasional Change	Ambiguous Changing

Job Description/Typical Day

The Project Manager deals with all facets of the development process, including, perhaps, site selection, architecture and engineering, contracting, lenders, and equity investors.

Life-style is heavily dependent upon project cyclicality. Pressure often builds with deadlines as a project progresses. This is a low-prestige job requiring one to deal with all levels of workers.

Skills

The position requires strong interpersonal skills, the ability to assess risk and deal with uncertainty, as well as entrepreneurial spirit; creativity; skills in financial analysis; the ability to initiate, coordinate, and negotiate; a project orientation; and the patience to deal with government agencies.

Typical Career Paths

MBAs usually begin as Assistant Project Managers for one or several projects, depending upon the company, before becoming Project Managers. Further advancement leads to bigger and/or more projects. At some point (two to ten years), the MBA may become a Partner, receiving equity in projects he or she manages. In other companies, the MBA does not participate in ownership, and, for example, may rise to a Vice-President, Commercial level and on up the corporate ladder to Executive VP and President.

REAL ESTATE: INDUSTRIAL BROKERS

Education (degrees)	BA	MBA	PhD
Experience required (yrs)	None	1-3	3+
Location	Urban	Rural	Regional / Travel
Compensation ($/yr)	< $25K	$25-30K	$30-35K / >$35K
Work involvement (hrs/wk)	< 50	50-60	> 60
Pace	Relaxed	Medium	Frenetic
Career path (a la Driver)	Spiral	Steady	Linear
Interpersonal style	Loner	Moderate	Outgoing
Cognitive style	Sequential Rules Details	Mixed Principles Systems	Random Free form Big picture
Variety (preference for)	No change Ordered	Occasional Change	Ambiguous Changing

INTRODUCTION

A major trend in the 1980s will be further attempts to draw together the frag-
mented brokerage industry. Opportunities will exist in large national franchises
(Century 21 and ERA), employee relocation services, computerized data systems,
and large new entrants (Merrill Lynch and Sears).

Job Description/Typical Day

Industrial Brokers find suitable land and buildings for industrial concerns.
Their duties include leasing and developing industrial property (e.g., industrial
parks) as well as listing and selling it. Entry into this field is slow and requires the
development of a client list. Hours are normal, and commissions are infrequent
but substantial.

Skills

The Industrial Broker must be familiar with industrial requirements and be
knowledgeable about local building, zoning, and tax laws. He or she must be able
to locate the pertinent facts and figures and then present them in a professional
manner to sophisticated business clients.

REAL ESTATE: COMMERCIAL BROKERS

Education (degrees)	BA	MBA	PhD
Experience required (yrs)	None	1-3	3+
Location	Urban	Rural	Regional / Travel
Compensation ($/yr)	$< $25K$	$25-30K	$30-35K / $>$35K
Work involvement (hrs/wk)	< 50	50-60	> 60
Pace	Relaxed	Medium	Frenetic
Career path (a la Driver)	Spiral	Steady	Linear
Interpersonal style	Loner	Moderate	Outgoing
Cognitive style	Sequential Rules Details	Mixed Principles Systems	Random Free form Big picture
Variety (preference for)	No change Ordered	Occasional Change	Ambiguous Changing

Sources of Additional Information

National Association of Home Builders
National Association of Real Estate Brokers
Society of Industrial Builders

Journals

Agency Sales
Buildings
Industrial Development
National Real Estate Investor
Professional Builders and Apartment Constructor News
Shopping Center World

39 RETAILING

	BA	MBA	PhD
Education (degrees)	BA	MBA	PhD
Experience required (yrs)	None	1-3	3+
Location	Urban	Rural	Regional / Travel
Compensation ($/yr)	< $25K	$25-30K	$30-35K / >$35K
Work involvement (hrs/wk)	< 50	50-60	> 60
Pace	Relaxed	Medium	Frenetic
Career path (a la Driver)	Spiral	Steady	Linear
Interpersonal style	Loner	Moderate	Outgoing
Cognitive style	Sequential Rules Details	Mixed Principles Systems	Random Free form Big picture
Variety (preference for)	No change Ordered	Occasional Change	Ambiguous Changing

INTRODUCTION

Retailing is the largest single industry in the United States, far bigger than second-place manufacturing. Retail sales represent 40 percent of the gross national product and 70 percent of Americans' disposable income. Retail employees account for 18 percent of the labor force in the United States, but earn 28.5 percent of the nation's wages and salaries. Considering the low pay associated with retailing's nonmanagement positions, this fact points out how well the retail executive is rewarded.

While the retailing field encompasses food, drug, and other chains, department stores are the predominant MBA recruiters.

Job Description/Typical Day

MBAs typically enter the merchandising (versus operations) side of retailing, as that is where department stores see the best utilization of MBA skills. Fast-track programs move the MBA from Assistant Buyer to Department Manager, and then to Buyer. The first two positions generally orient the employee to merchandising and store culture and involve a great deal of "grunt work."

The department store Buyer is involved with advertising, merchandising, and promotion decisions, but primarily has responsibility for buying stock for his or her department. A Buyer generally selects merchandise for more than one store and, therefore, must know the demographics, population size, square footages, and so on, for various stores in his or her territory. The Buyer must be able to work with the sales representatives of various manufacturers and with his or her own company's fashion office for information on what to buy. The Buyer has the final word on what will be sold through his or her departments.

Any potential entrant to the field must be aware of the demanding time commitment. At a minimum, a Buyer works a floating five-and-a-half day workweek from a 9-to-6 daily schedule, minimum. The rule is longer hours and, at Christmas time six-day, 9-to-9 schedules are commonplace.

From a position of Buyer, the MBA can progress into general merchandise management or store management. The Merchandise Manager is responsible for the development of merchandising programs in the store and for a knowledge of quality, customer utility, price position, sales volumes, gross margins, and competitive pricing. Duties include the development of sales tools (literature, manuals, etc.), recommendation of new products, sales volume projections, and an analysis of trade information. The role of a Merchandise Manager is becoming that of a specialist in the distribution of goods versus one of supervisor of salespeople and tracker of inventories.

Skills

There are five skills necessary to do well in major department store retailing. They are, in order of importance:

Interpersonal Skills. Retailing is a people-intensive business. You will deal with large numbers of people with widely varying degrees of skill and importance. You will have frequent and intense contact with supervisors, suppliers, peers, and subordinates—including legions of clerks. Everyone's support will be necessary, and the typical quasi-matrix organization will make good interpersonal skills crucial.

The Ability to React Quickly. Decisions are made often and fast. Strategic planning, if any, will be an annual or semiannual event. To borrow a term from boxing, you will be a hands-on "counterpuncher," and not making two-to-five year plans.

Organizational Ability. You will have many different irons in the fire at any one time. You will need to arrange your time and efforts so that you will be able to do *most* of your tasks well.

Analytical Ability. You will need to apply some of your (recently?) learned analytical skills. While this is a relatively recent addition to the list, it is becoming increasingly important and retailers are more willing to pay for it.

Risk-Taking Ability. A buyer is necessarily always planning and buying anywhere from 6 to 12 months ahead. A commitment of $100,000 for a style different from this year's trend involves confidence in one's predictive skills regarding next season's "success."

Compensation

For the 12 1980 Harvard Business School graduates hired into retailing, the mean salary was $30,541 versus $32,484 for the class as a whole. The retailing range was $22,500 to $48,500. However, retailing salaries soon catch up and often surpass those in other MBA-hiring industries. MBAs are given quite a bit of responsibility in the first few years, with salary increases tied directly to individual performance. Top MBA salaries will normally at least double in three to five years. Benefits are good, often including a shopping discount of up to 20 percent.

Typical Career Paths

Most careers in retailing start with a training program that exposes the MBA to both buying and store operations. Many retailers have special "fast-track" programs that enable an MBA to become a buyer within 15 to 24 months. However, they expect that an MBA *will* progress quickly and thus make profits for them quickly. The message is clearly "up or out." After two to three years of exposure to all aspects of retailing, you must choose to continue in buying/merchandising or store operations or in a staff function (control, finance, MIS, etc.). Using the Bloomingdale's program as an example, the following career progression can be expected.

Orientation	3 months
Assistant buyer in New York	6 months
Branch store department manager	6 to 12 months
New York store department manager	6 to 12 months
Branch store merchandise manager	6 to 12 months
Continue in store operations, buying, or staff position	

If you continue in the buying function, you can expect to remain there for five to seven years before becoming an Administrator (in charge of seven to nine buyers). During those years, you will assume responsibility for more departments and add to your volume (and compensation).

An option open to a Buyer after one or two years is to switch to another chain, switch sides and become a Manufacturer's Representative, or buy for an individual store.

Some Employers

Some large retailers, such as Sears (Chicago) or Woolworth (New York) are hiring few MBAs, while others, such as Dayton-Hudson (Minneapolis), Bloomingdale's (New York), and Macy's (New York) are committed to hiring them. The Chairmen of Bloomingdale's and Macy's are both Harvard Business School graduates.

Major Ownership Groups of Traditional Department Stores

Allied Stores (New York, New York): Jordan Marsh, Read's, Miller & Rhoads, Ann Taylor, Garfinkel's, among others.

Associated Dry Goods (New York, New York): Lord & Taylor; J.W. Robertson Co.; L.S. Ayres and Company; Sibley, Lindsay & Curr Co.; among others.

Federated Department Stores (Cincinnati,Ohio): A & S, Bloomingdale's, Filene's

R.H. Macy & Co. (New York, New York): Macy's, Bamberger's, Davison's

May Department Stores (St. Louis, Missouri): Venture, G. Fox

Dayton-Hudson (Minneapolis, Minnesota): Dayton's

Specialty Stores

Cole National Corp. (Billings, Montana)

Edison Brothers (St. Louis, Missouri) Clothes and shoes

Gap stores (San Bruno, California)

Others

Jewel Companies (Chicago, Illinois)

K Mart Corp. (Troy, Michigan)

Additional Information

Emphasis that one Buyer expressed was on the "willingness to put in the hours—and enjoy it." This buyer's most frustrating task was the volume of paperwork necessary. The most rewarding aspect was the ability to walk into a store "and see me—my goods, my displays, and my plan—all moving!"

Sources of Additional Information:

Chain Store Age

College Placement Annual, 1980 (listing of retailers)

"The *Fortune* Directory of the Largest Non-Industrial Companies," *Fortune,* July 14, 1980 (listing of the fifty largest retailing companies ranked by sales)

"$100 Million Club," *Chain Store Age Executive*, August 1980, (listing of retailers comparing stores in existence and being planned, as well as comparative sales figures)

"Retail Distribution," *Forbes*, January 7, 1980 (listing of discount and variety stores, and specialty retailers)

"Top 100 Stores: The Big Winners," *Stores*, July 1979 (ranking of the top 100 department store divisions by 1978 volume)

There is an interesting article by Elizabeth G. Hirschman and Ronald W. Stampel in the *Journal of Retailing*, Vol. 56, no. 1 (Spring 1980), entitled "Role of Retailing in the Diffusion of Popular Culture: Microperspectives."

The industry is experiencing explosive growth due to liberal changes in tax laws. Investors' interest in venture capital is increasing due to decreasing returns on more traditional investments.

Sources of Additional Information

McKIERNAN, JOHN. *Planning and Financing Your New Business: A Guide to Venture Capital*, Chestnut Hill, Massachusetts: Technology Management, 1978.
PRATT, STANLEY E., *Guide to Venture Capital Sources*, New York: Scribner, 1982.

Education (degrees)	BA	MBA	PhD
Experience required (yrs)	None	1-3	3+
Location	Urban	Rural	Regional / Travel
Compensation ($/yr)	< $25K	$25-30K	$30-35K / >$35K
Work involvement (hrs/wk)	< 50	50-60	> 60
Pace	Relaxed	Medium	Frenetic
Career path (a la Driver)	Spiral	Steady	Linear
Interpersonal style	Loner	Moderate	Outgoing
Cognitive style	Sequential Rules Details	Mixed Principles Systems	Random Free form Big picture
Variety (preference for)	No change Ordered	Occasional Change	Ambiguous Changing

Job Description/Typical Day

The activities vary according to whom you work for within an administration and for which administration you work. Major areas within White House Staff include National Security Council, Council of Economic Advisors, Domestic Policy Staff, Office of Science and Technology Policy, Counsel, Press Secretary, Congressional Liaison, Speechwriters, and others. Examples of tasks include preparing and doing advance work for presidential trips, preparing presidential decision papers, and working with various agencies to see if policies are being implemented in accord with the President's wishes.

The White House staff position has been described as a "firefighter" in that it is not for those who prefer to work with one task to its completion without interruption. This can be considered an advantage, however, for those who like variety in their work. The amount of travel varies from a few days to many months per year depending upon the job.

The job is emotionally and physically draining. Long hours are required, at least six days a week including "office hours," and there are frequent work-related social events. Few vacation days are taken other than those absolutely needed for rest or "mental health."

Skills

The specific skills needed vary with the specific assignment. Higher-level staff stresses political skills and the ability to get along with others in an often highly pressured situation. Lower-level and more staff-related tasks require writing skills, with political skills far less important.

Typical Career Paths

White House Staff positions are often transitory. Some National Security and Economic Advisor people keep popping up year after year. Others must leave when the President does.

After working on staff all of those interviewed reported vastly broadened options and a much larger network of connections among high-level people. Interviewees moved on into a variety of fields—private enterprise, public administration, academia, and nonprofit.

There are three major ways to get on the White House Staff, according to a former staffer in the Kennedy Administration:

1. Back a politician through thick and thin and hope he wins. He will always reward those who stuck by him "when no one else believed." That takes luck.
2. Become a White House Fellow. However, only 15 to 20 of these are accepted per year out of thousands of applicants. Currently, a 50:50 male/female ratio is accepted. Candidates should be young professionals with strong track records. Hence, people right out of school are not the most likely to get in. Even among those accepted, only about four work in the White House or Executive Office. The rest work with the cabinets and agencies—but all at relatively high levels.

3. Become an expert, and a visible expert, through publications, media, organizational, or personal connection in an area salient to government priority decision making.

Additional Information

White House Fellows come from the private sector. They are discouraged from staying on after their year is up. While many continue for months or even a year or more afterwards, they usually leave and go back to the private sector.

However, the contacts made through their year are invaluable, and all those interviewed reported having had their options greatly widened. They reported having a large number of offers to choose from upon leaving and have gone on to work in corporations, in academia, and in other government positions. Fellows also have a strong alumni network.

Applying for the program, prospective fellows are asked to demonstrate how the year with government will enhance their contribution to their existing vocation.

JOB RESEARCH REPORT UPDATES

We expect that as you read the Job Research Reports, you will find data that you know are outdated or perhaps different from your experience. This is a function of the way in which the book was written, relying on the substantial but diverse talents and perspectives of hundreds of students in two institutions. We encourage you, therefore, to use the succeeding pages to suggest changes in the next edition. You may even wish to suggest an additional title or two. We look forward to hearing from you and will certainly acknowledge your contribution.

JOB RESEARCH REPORT UPDATE

Here is some information that you really ought to include in your next edition:

Your Name: _____ Telephone: _____

Your Address: _____

Your Experience/Job Title: _____
Suggestions on the book or its structure overall:

Suggestions on the Job Research Reports:

Job Title: _____

Job Description/Typical Day:

Necessary Skills:

Typical Career Paths:

Compensation:

Some Employers:

Sources of Additional Information:

JOB RESEARCH REPORT UPDATE

Here is some information that you really ought to include in your next edition:

Your Name: _____ Telephone: _____

Your Address: _____

Your Experience/Job Title: _____
Suggestions on the book or its structure overall:

Suggestions on the Job Research Reports:

Job Title: _____

Job Description/Typical Day:

Necessary Skills:

Typical Career Paths:

Compensation:

Some Employers:

Sources of Additional Information:

JOB RESEARCH REPORT UPDATE

Here is some information that you really ought to include in your next edition:

Your Name: _____ Telephone: _____

Your Address: _____

Your Experience/Job Title: _____
Suggestions on the book or its structure overall:

Suggestions on the Job Research Reports:

Job Title: _____

Job Description/Typical Day:

Necessary Skills:

Typical Career Paths:

Compensation:

Some Employers:

Sources of Additional Information:

Personal Job Search Profile Card

for _____   (Date: /   /   )

	BA	MBA	PhD
Education (degrees)	BA	MBA	PhD
Experience required (yrs)	None	1-3	3+
Location	Urban	Rural	Regional / Travel
Compensation ($/yr)	$< $25K$	$25-30K	$30-35K / $>$35K
Work involvement (hrs/wk)	$<$ 50	50-60	$>$ 60
Pace	Relaxed	Medium	Frenetic
Career path (a la Driver)	Spiral	Steady	Linear
Interpersonal style	Loner	Moderate	Outgoing
Cognitive style	Sequential Rules Details	Mixed Principles Systems	Random Free form Big picture
Variety (preference for)	No change Ordered	Occasional change	Ambiguous Changing

NOTES

NOTES